# UML REQUIREMENTS MODELING FOR BUSINESS ANALYSTS

first edition

# NORMAN DAOUST

Published by:
**Technics Publications, LLC**
966 Woodmere Drive
Westfield, NJ 07090 U.S.A.
www.technicspub.com
Edited by Carol Lehn
Cover design by Mark Brye

This book is printed on acid-free paper.

ISBN, print ed.        978-1-9355042-4-5

First Printing 2012

Library of Congress Control Number: 2012943403

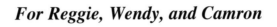

*For Reggie, Wendy, and Camron*

# Contents

# List of Figures

# List of Tables

# Acknowledgements

Thanks for choosing this book. My wish is that the ideas and techniques presented help you as much as they have helped me.

I hope you find yourself using these guidelines and tips over and over again, until they become ingrained habits that enable you to work both more quickly and with better results.

Thanks to Steve Hoberman for encouraging me to write this book, and to Barbara von Halle for her inspiration during the extensive revision process for the draft versions. Thank you to the Cambridge Public Library for providing a place and atmosphere conducive to thinking and writing. Many thanks are due to the extremely knowledgeable readers who provided numerous ideas, suggestions, and improvements: Susan Burk; Karen L. Dawson, MBA; Ed Landale; Bil Lewis; Charlie Mead; and Nathaniel Packard, CBAP. Kudos to Carol Lean, the editor who asked many excellent questions that are now answered in the text.

I've been fortunate to have had excellent teachers along the road of life. They include Mrs. Rodgers, Peter Martinelli, Gil French, and Roger Douglass. The people and sources I've picked up modeling ideas from are too numerous to mention. However I will give special thanks to my primary modeling mentors, even though they never volunteered for that role: Abdul-Malik Shakir and the inimitable Linda Quade.

Norman Daoust
Cambridge, MA, USA
www.DaoustAssociates.com
June 1, 2012

Are you thinking to yourself, "Why should I learn these models, diagrams, and techniques?" If so, one or more of these reasons may apply to you:

- To communicate more succinctly and effectively with your stakeholders, including your software development team
- To increase the likelihood that your requirements will be reviewed and understood
- To make your job easier
- To set you apart from your peers
- To enhance your tool set with powerful diagramming techniques
- To make it easier for others to catch any omissions and errors your requirements might have, in less time and earlier in the project lifecycle
- To support the testing process and authoring of a user guide
- To document requirements in a manner that facilitates traceability to architecture and implementation artifacts
- To understand system designs and documentation which utilize the Unified Modeling Language (UML) notation.

## Intended Audience

If you're a business analyst seeking practical advice and guidance to capture and document requirements, or are interested in requirements modeling using UML or use cases, this book is for you! If you are a manager of business analysts, this book is also for you, since it will serve as your reference guide for assisting your business analysts in becoming more effective in their requirements analysis efforts.

## Scope

But first, what it's not. This book will not teach you all the details of UML. There are several excellent reference books available to describe UML in considerable detail. I heartily recommend those books for anyone interested in the technical details, theoretical framework, or the metamodel underlying UML. For a superb overview of UML, I enthusiastically recommend Martin Fowler's *UML Distilled* [Fowler, 2004]: it's short, to the point, and easily comprehensible. For the technical details, go to the source, the UML specifications [UML Infrastructure 2.4.1] and [UML Superstructure

2.4.1]. Instead, this book provides information on the 20% of the UML that you'll use to document more than 80% of the requirements.

This book is about requirements and analysis; it is <u>not</u> about technical design, development, and testing of software systems. UML provides many diagrams and tools for the design and implementation phases of the software development life cycle, but explaining how the UML diagrams are used for technical design, development, and testing of software systems is not what this book covers.

This book will not teach you how to use any of the UML software tools. There are user guides, web sites, and training courses that do that quite well. Just reading this book will not instantly turn you into an excellent modeler. However, continual practice and feedback will help you achieve that goal. Instead, this book provides you with a plethora of best practices, guidelines, and tips, as well as some common pitfalls to avoid when utilizing UML for business analysis purposes. The contents have been assembled over the years based on experience, feedback, and documented best practices. This guide can help you focus your attention on the simple steps you can take to improve your modeling efforts. You can apply all of these ideas immediately.

While I often list various options, I include my recommended choices and opinions when I think you'll benefit. Organizations will typically adapt these guidelines to fit both their needs and their environment.

If you're a neophyte modeler, this book will enable you to learn good habits from the beginning. If you're an experienced modeler, it will likely make concrete some of the practices you may already use unconsciously, as well as provide you with new ideas that will become part of your standard operating procedure in future modeling efforts.

You will rarely find this type of information in books. Experts learn these over time and use them in their work practices, but seldom share them in book form.

Some people do things better because they do things differently. My hope is that from now on you will model differently by using these standard diagrams and models and applying the tips and guidelines to become more productive and produce better quality models in less time.

## *Organization of This Book*

This book is organized so you can quickly find your topic of interest from a brief glance at the Table of Contents, the list of figures, which lists all the example diagrams, or the list of tables, which includes all the tables containing the diagram icons for business analysis use.

There are several brief introductory chapters:

- Chapter 2 UML Modeling for Business Analysis: This presents reasons for utilizing Unified Modeling Language (UML) for business analysis, a brief history of the Unified Modeling Language, and the categories of diagrams it contains.
- Chapter 3 General UML Diagram Guidelines: This provides a set of general modeling guidelines and tips applicable to all the UML diagrams.
- Chapter 4 Example Model Introduction: This provides a brief overview of a fictitious Somestate Department of Motor Vehicles example that is used throughout the book.

Following those is a chapter for each of the thirteen UML diagram types. The diagram types are presented in the following order:

- Chapter 5 Use Case Models: Use Case models are the most frequently used UML model type for business analysts.
- Chapter 6 Activity Diagrams: Activity diagrams are a powerful tool for process modeling; think of them as flow charts, possibly on steroids.
- Chapter 7 Interaction Overview Diagrams: Interaction Overview diagrams are seldom used for business analysis, however they are helpful occasionally. They have functionality similar to Activity diagrams plus more.
- Chapter 8 Class Models: Class models are powerful tools for business analysis purposes because in a single diagram, they combine both data requirements and behavior requirements, the actions performed on the classes.
- Chapter 9 Object Diagrams. Object diagrams should be used whenever Class diagrams or data model diagrams are used to make the concepts in Class models and data models more concrete to your readers.
- Chapter 10 State Machine Models: State Machine models are simple but powerful tools for illustrating lifecycles. They should be used more frequently in business analysis.

- Chapter 11 Timing Diagrams: Timing diagrams serve a useful purpose by illustrating in a diagram format the business rules involving timing relationships, time durations, or time constraints between different states of an object or between the state transitions of different objects. They are typically not used for business analysis purposes. However, they do come in handy on occasion.
- Chapter 12 Sequence Diagrams: Sequence diagrams illustrate the time sequence of the information exchanges between various systems.
- Chapter 13 Communication Diagrams: Communication diagrams show a summary of the flow of information between various systems.
- Chapter 14 Composite Structure Diagrams: Since these are used to represent software classes, they are typically not used for business analysis purposes. While you'll never need to create this diagram type for requirements purposes, they are used as part of system design or documentation. Therefore they are included so you will be able to recognize them and understand them.
- Chapter 15 Component Diagrams: Since these are used to represent software components, they're typically not used for business analysis purposes. While you'll never need to create this diagram type for requirements purposes, they are used as part of system design or documentation. Therefore they are included so you will be able to recognize them and understand them.
- Chapter 16 Deployment Diagrams: Since these are used to represent software files resident on specific hardware, they're typically not used for business analysis purposes. While you'll never need to create this diagram type for requirements purposes, they are used as part of system design or documentation. Therefore they are included so you will be able to recognize them and understand them.
- Chapter 17 Package Diagrams: Package diagrams are used to break up large models and diagrams into smaller, more manageable portions.

These thirteen UML diagram types are followed by chapters for two additional diagram types that are included as techniques in the Business Analysis Body of Knowledge (BABOK), important for business analysts, and that can be created using UML notation:

- Chapter 18 Context Diagrams Using Communication Diagram Notation: This describes the use of Communication diagram notation for creating Context diagrams.

- Chapter 19 Data Models Using Class Diagram Notation: This describes the use of Class diagram notation for data modeling.

Each of the previously mentioned chapters for a diagram type includes the following sections, allowing you to quickly locate the specific information you're looking for:

- Introduction: This section provides an informal definition of the diagram type, what the diagram type contains, and whether it's included in the Business Analysis Body of Knowledge.
- Purpose: This section describes why and when you would want to use this diagram type.
- Guidelines: This section describes what the diagrams are useful and appropriate for, and under what circumstances you would use them.
- Diagram Notation: This section lists the diagram elements business analysts should recognize. While there are many others included in the UML specifications, those are deliberately not included in this book, since business analysts will seldom encounter them. For information on these, see *UML Distilled* [Fowler, 2004] and [UML Superstructure 2.4.1]. Within this section, the diagram elements are listed in the following order:
  a) diagram "nodes", in the UML specifications these are called "graphic nodes"; think of them as the icons to focus on
  b) diagram connectors, in the UML specifications these are called "graphic paths"; think of them as the lines that connect the diagram "nodes"
  c) diagram containment elements; think of these as containers for grouping together the other categories of diagram elements
  d) diagram other; these are not diagram icons as are the other categories, but time and duration text annotations that can appear in several diagram types

Within those categories, the diagram elements are listed in alphabetical order. Not all diagram types include diagram elements from all four categories; only the relevant categories are included in each chapter.

For each diagram element there is an image of the diagram icon, the UML name of that icon, an informal definition, suggestions for use, and a list of UML diagram types in which the icon would be used for business analysis purpose, and if the icon is not included in the first diagram of the Diagram Examples section of the chapter, a reference to a diagram that includes the icon.

- Diagram Examples: This section includes one or more examples of the diagram. Throughout the book, the examples and diagrams have been created to be understandable and to illustrate specific UML modeling concepts. They are not necessarily intended to be complete or illustrative of the complexity of the real world.
- Diagram Tips: This section includes tips for creating and laying out the diagram type.
- How-to-Model Tips: This section includes tips on modeling the diagram type.
- Naming Guidelines: This section includes conventions for naming the items in the diagram so that your models are both consistent and easy for your readers to understand.
- Modeling Process Summary: This section provides a summary of a process to create the model or diagram type.
- Case Study Example Diagram: This section demonstrates how you can describe to your stakeholders the example diagram type from the Case Study.
- Relationship to Other UML Diagrams: This section describes relationships between elements of this diagram and those of the other UML diagram types.

Those chapters are followed by Chapter 20 Which Diagrams Do I Create and When? This provides tips on which diagrams to create first and under what conditions you would create each of the diagram types.

Chapter 21 Case Study presents a case study, describing the modeling process for creating the sample diagrams and models, and highlighting the relationships between aspects of the different models.

The Appendixes include:

- Appendix A Glossary: This includes terms used throughout the book. Look here for definitions of terms not defined elsewhere in the book.
- Appendix B Grammar Summary for Modelers: This provides a brief summary of the grammatical terms referenced in the Naming Guidelines sections of the main chapters.
- Appendix C Analysis Datatypes: This includes a list of analysis datatypes for use in Class models and data models for business analysis purposes. Analysis datatypes are used to categorize attributes in the Class Models and Data Models Using Class Diagram Notation chapters.

- Appendix D References: This includes the list of books, articles, and web sites referenced throughout the book.

## How to Use This Book

There are several ways to use this book, depending on your experience and your immediate needs.

- If you're familiar with modeling and have specific questions or issues for a particular diagram type or model, locate the appropriate chapter from the Table of Contents and then skim the sections of that chapter to find your answer or obtain guidelines or hints. This will likely take you less than five minutes. Alternately, if you have questions about a particular diagram type, review the Table of Figures to see if one of the example diagrams will answer your question; if so, go directly to that example diagram.
- If you're relatively new to modeling and have a particular question or challenge, first review the Table of Contents, and briefly read the Introduction and Purpose sections at the beginning of each of the thirteen chapters for a UML model or diagram type. Then for the chapter of the diagram type or model you're initially most interested in, first glance at the example diagrams in the Diagram Examples and Case Study Example Diagram sections, then glance briefly through the various chapter sections, and give the chapter a quick read. This will both provide you with immediate information and familiarize you with the structure of the other chapters. All of this should take about twenty minutes.
- If you're not familiar with UML and would like an overview, first read the Introduction, then review the Table of Contents, then for each of the thirteen chapters for a UML model or diagram type, read the Introduction and Purpose sections and briefly glance at the Diagram Examples and Case Study Example Diagram sections. This will provide you with a brief overview in about twenty-five minutes. Then you can spend time reviewing the chapter that's of most interest.

Each of you will have additional tips and guidelines that you'll develop. Write them right in the book at the appropriate location. If you think your tips would be helpful to others, email them to the author. If your idea is used and you're the first one to suggest it, you'll receive recognition on the web site.

## *Terminology*

### MODEL

In this book, the term model is sometimes used to refer to the entire collection of UML diagrams and their associated text for a business or system that is the subject of the analysis. Thus a model of a state's Department of Motor Vehicles system might include three Use Case diagrams (one for vehicle registrations, one for driver's licenses, and one for motor vehicle titles), three Class diagrams, several Object diagrams, several State Machine diagrams, several Sequence diagrams and a Communication diagram. However in several cases, specifically Use Case model, Class model, and State Machine model, the term model is used to refer to the multiple diagrams (and their associated text) of those diagram types, since those diagram types frequently require more one diagram. I chose to simply write "Use Case model" rather than "the multiple Use Case diagrams and their associated text needed for your business or system under analysis". For example, we would refer to the Use Case model of a state's Department of Motor Vehicles system to reference all three Use Case diagrams (and their associated text): Vehicle Registration Use Case diagram, Driver's License Use Case diagram, and Vehicle Title Use Case diagram. It should be clear from the context which definition is being used.

### DIAGRAM VERSUS TEXT VERSUS MODEL

A diagram is a graphical representation of a model. There are also text representations of the same model and sometimes table versions, as well. For example, both a diagram version and a table version of the same State Machine are included in the State Machine Models chapter. Strictly speaking, all diagram types have associated text. In practice, the associated text is very important for Use Case and Class models; some of the other diagram types seldom have associated text. In this book, when we refer to a diagram type, we generally mean the diagram type and its associated text. In some organizations, only the diagram is created when it is self-explanatory without the associated text. The amount of associated text you'll include is dependent on your organization's policies and software development lifecycle methodology. Some organizations require extensive text documentation in a specific format; others require less documentation, and thus self-explanatory diagrams may be sufficient for the intended purposes, particularly when using agile methodologies.

### DIAGRAM TYPE VERSUS DIAGRAM

There are thirteen UML diagram types. Each example diagram in this book is one diagram of the applicable UML diagram type. To avoid continually writing "... diagram of diagram type ...", the book frequently uses "... diagram" to mean "a specific diagram of the type …". Thus, you'll read "Use an Activity diagram to visually illustrate decisions, branching, and the sequence of actions in a process." instead of "Use a specific diagram of the type Activity diagram to visually illustrate decisions, branching, and the sequence of actions in a process."

## TYPE VERSUS INSTANCE

A state Department of Motor Vehicles keeps records of motor vehicles. My car is an instance of (or is one occurrence of) a motor vehicle. UML includes the concept of both a Class diagram, which includes "types", and an Object diagram, which includes "instances". An object is just an instance of a class. For example, if the class is Person, "Jane Doe", as an instance of a person, would be an Object.

## *Stylistic Conventions*

The thirteen UML diagram types are capitalized throughout the text (e.g., Use Case diagram).

Capitalization is used in the following three cases where a single UML model type consists of more than one diagram: Use Case model, Class model, and State Machine model.

Generally, the UML diagram element names are capitalized throughout the text when referring to UML icons (e.g., Actor icon, Association icon, Class icon, Object Node icon, Use Case icon). The same terms are generally not capitalized when referring to the general concept of the same name (e.g. class, use case).

References to figures and tables use a different font (e.g., `Figure 5-1 vehicle registration`, `UML Use Case diagram: system use case`, `Table 5-1 Use Case Diagram Notation`). The name of each figure and diagram includes the UML diagram type (e.g., `Figure 5-1 vehicle registration`, `UML Use Case diagram: system use case`). In the text explanations that accompany the diagram examples, the values that appear in the diagrams are italicized. For example, the text explanation of `Figure 5-1 vehicle registration`, `UML Use Case diagram: system use case` is "`Figure 5-1 vehicle registration`, `UML Use Case diagram: system use case`, a system perspective UML Use Case diagram, indicates that a *registration administrator* initiates the *issue vehicle registration* use case, and also initiates the use case *renew vehicle registration* use case. …" Each of the italicized terms can be found as values for particular diagram elements (e.g., Actor names and Use Case names in the previous sentence) or other items in the referenced diagram.

## And After Reading This Book?

Unfortunately, just reading this book won't make you a better modeler. To do that, you must take action. You must use the information, the tips, and the guidelines regularly until they become ingrained habits that allow you to work smarter and quicker and achieve higher quality results.

Keep in mind Aristotle's pointed observation, "We are what we repeatedly do. Excellence, then, is not an act, but a habit."

Utilize these guidelines daily and become an excellent modeler!

## Feedback

Additional information and any detected errata will be provided at www.DaoustAssociates.com. That site includes instructions to contact the author.

Feel free to contact us for clarification, comments, and criticisms. We welcome them all! If you agree with these ideas or found them useful, we'd love to hear about that. If you disagree, we'd like to understand why.

## About the Author

Norman Daoust is a business analyst trainer, requirements modeler, data modeler, healthcare electronic data exchange specialist, fretted instrument specialist, and organic gardener. He is the principal consultant for Daoust Associates, www.DaoustAssociates.com, a company based in Cambridge, Massachusetts, United States. He specializes in business analyst training, data modeling, requirements modeling, and healthcare systems integration.

Norman's clients have included the Centers for Disease Control and Prevention, the Clinical Data Interchange Standards Consortium, the Canadian Institute for Health Information, Partners HealthCare Systems, the Veterans Health Administration, several high tech startups, and a Fortune 500 software company. In 2010, Health Level Seven International named Norman Daoust as one of twenty-five people in the world to receive their inaugural HL7 Fellowship award. An active member for more than fifteen years, Norman was honored for his outstanding service, commitment, and contributions to the international healthcare standards organization.

You may be thinking, "I already create requirements documents using text, tables, and perhaps some diagrams and flow charts. Why should I use UML?"

And you may know that UML, with the exception of Use Case models, was not designed for business analysis. It was primarily targeted toward software designers and software developers. However the world has changed since 1997 (when UML was first published) and so have the uses of UML.

Here are several reasons to utilize UML as part of requirements analysis and documentation:

- Several of the UML diagrams are referenced in *Business Analysis Body of Knowledge* (BABOK) [BABOK 2.0]: Use Case, Class, State Machine (referred to in the BABOK as State Diagram), Activity, and Sequence diagrams.[1]
- UML is a standard widely used throughout the world and across many industries.
- UML has widespread tool support.
- UML can easily be used for purposes other than it was designed for. For example, Class models can be used for data modeling (as mentioned in the BABOK), and Communication diagram notation can be used to create Context diagrams.
- A picture is more valuable than a thousand words when your stakeholders need an overview.
- But most importantly, UML can make your requirements more precise, easier to review, easier to understand, and more compact, and thus more valuable.

However, you should be aware that because many software developers are only familiar with its use for software design and software documentation, when they initially read your UML analysis models, some may interpret your analysis models as software designs, and some may critique your models as "incorrect" or suggest that you use more specific UML constructs (e.g., aggregation or composition, rather than your regular associations in Class models).

---

[1] The author has recommended that Object diagrams be included in the next version of the BABOK for reasons described in Chapter 9 Object Diagrams.

To deal with these challenges, you may:

- Explicitly label your models as analysis models.
- Explain to them you're using UML for analysis purposes, not for the software design or software documentation they may be used to creating or reading.
- Refer them to *UML Distilled* [Fowler, 2004], where Martin Fowler describes three typical ways UML is used- as a sketch, as a blueprint, and as a programming language. Then explain you're using UML as a blueprint for requirements analysis purposes.

## UML History

The first version of Unified Modeling Language was published in 1997, although a preliminary version was released in 1995. It has undergone several revisions, the most recent as of this writing is version 2.4.1.

With the exception of use cases, the original UML version was used primarily for software design, development, and documentation. The other diagrams were seldom used for business analysis except by a relatively small number of early adopters.

That has changed over time. Five of the thirteen UML diagram types are referenced in the BABOK Version 2.0. This book recommends another and describes how the UML notation can be adapted to create Context diagrams and data models.

The vast majority of the material in this book will also apply to future versions of the UML for several reasons: many of the guidelines and tips are generic and not dependent on specific details of the UML, the percentage of the UML that is applicable for business analysis is quite small, and the majority of changes to the UML have been to enhance its usefulness for design and implementation. This book was written based on Version 2.3. No changes were needed when Version 2.4.1 was published.

## UML Diagram Categories

The UML specifications [UML Superstructure 2.4.1] classify the UML diagrams at the top-most level into two categories. `Figure 2-1 UML diagram categories, UML Class diagram` indicates that at the top most level there are two categories of *UML diagrams*: *Structure diagrams* and *Behavior diagrams*. Structure diagrams contain the static elements of a system. Behavior diagrams illustrate the dynamic elements of a system and illustrate changes and events over time.

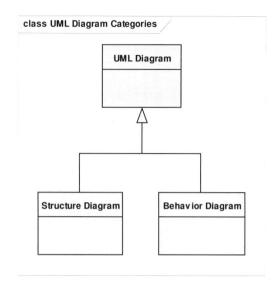

**Figure 2-1 UML diagram categories, UML Class diagram**

Figure 2-2 UML structural diagrams, UML Class diagram indicates that *Structure diagrams* are further categorized into *Class diagrams*, *Object diagrams*, *Composite Structure diagrams*, *Component diagrams*, *Deployment diagrams*, and *Package diagrams*.

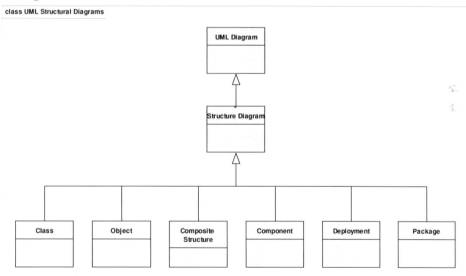

**Figure 2-2 UML structural diagrams, UML Class diagram**

Figure 2-3 UML behavior diagrams, UML Class diagram indicates that *Behavior diagrams* can be categorized into *Use Case diagrams*, *Activity diagrams*, *State Machine diagrams* and a category called *Interaction diagrams*. Included in the interaction category are *Sequence diagrams, Communication diagrams, Interaction Overview diagrams,* and *Timing diagrams.*

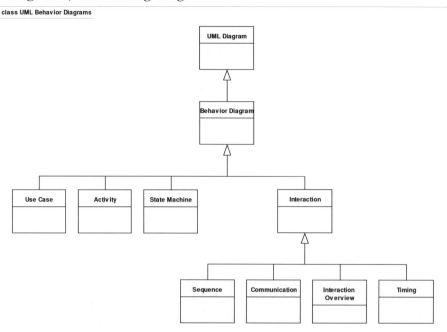

**Figure 2-3 UML behavior diagrams, UML Class diagram**

Each of the thirteen diagram types describes a business or system from a different viewpoint. Your target audience, purpose, and scope of your project will determine which of the diagram types will be appropriate for your project.

These categories are helpful. Each of the diagram types has certain diagram elements that are typically used in diagrams of that type. Diagram types of a given category tend to share typical diagram elements with other diagram types in that category, more so than with diagram types of a different category. However, UML does not prohibit including any of the diagram elements typically found in any of the diagram types in a diagram of a different type. Thus you could place an Interaction Use icon, typically used only in diagram types of the Interaction category, into a Use Case diagram. However these non-typical diagram elements are likely to either confuse your readers or at least require an explanation, thus the author generally recommends not using them. Fortunately, each diagram has "typical" diagram elements that are generally found in that diagram. The individual chapters list the author's recommendation of "typical" diagram elements to use for business analysis purposes. Stick to those typical diagram elements to improve the understanding and readability of your diagrams. However, when appropriate for accomplishing your goal, you can go outside the typical diagram element set.

This chapter includes information applicable to all UML diagram types.

## *Guidelines*

The most important advice I can give is to always keep in mind the following three aspects of your modeling situation:

- <u>T</u>arget <u>A</u>udience
- <u>P</u>urpose
- <u>S</u>cope

Following this Daoust Associates TAPS guideline will ensure that no one ever plays "Taps"[2] over your model.

Your target audience will determine the level of detail you present as well as the terminology you use. Is your target audience the business sponsor, business stakeholders, the software development team, other business analysts?

Know your target audience and model appropriately. For example, if the intended audience is domain or subject matter experts, use terms familiar to them and avoid technical terms.

Include the appropriate amount of information in a model. Typically this means include only relevant information. If your target audience is software developers who focus on technical details, include the technical details; if not, leave them out.

The purpose of the model will assist in determining the scope and level of detail, as well as which of the UML diagrams you include. Is it to document an existing system, to document the requirements of a future system, to document the current business process, to document the future business process? Is it to meet your organization's deliverable requirements, to provide the contract between the business stakeholders and the software development team, to provide an initial communication vehicle to serve as the focus of further conversations with the software development team?

---

[2] "Taps" is the name of the musical selection typically played on bugle or trumpet at the conclusion of a military funeral in the United States.

Martin Fowler says people use UML for three different purposes: sketch, blueprint, and programming language [Fowler, 2004]. Your purpose and target audience determine the appropriate level of detail, depth, and rigor for your model. When using a UML diagram as a sketch, it may be informal, incomplete, and only hand-written on a whiteboard or flip chart to communicate with your audience members at that point in time. This is a typical use in agile methodologies. When using a UML diagram as a blueprint, it will be more complete, formal, created with a software tool, and used as a requirements deliverable. Blueprint is the purpose this book addresses. UML is used as a programming language only by systems designers and developers, and will involve usage of a tool and program code generation.

Model <u>only</u> what's in scope. If you begin modeling outside the scope of the project, the entire world becomes the subject of your modeling efforts and your lifetime becomes the likely completion deadline.[3] Several of the diagram types are well suited to providing a visual representation of scope: Context diagram, Use Case diagram, and Activity diagram (when created at an overview level). Use these to assist in clarifying the scope when it's not clear, and to visual demonstrate it to reinforce the scope.

Remember the Daoust Associates modeling rule of thumb: make certain your model is "as simple as possible, but no simpler"[4] to suit its specified purpose.

### Diagram Notation

The UML specification [UML Superstructure 2.4.1] lists those diagram elements and connectors typically used in a given UML diagram type. However, the specification does not disallow any diagram element in any of the UML diagram types. In this book the Diagram Notation section for each UML diagram type lists the subset of those diagram elements and icons that the author recommends business analysts use

---

[3] When creating Use Case models, Alistair Cockburn recommends keeping a two column "In/Out list" of use cases: the "In" column contains those use cases that are in scope, the "Out" column contains those use cases that are out of scope. Consider maintaining an Out of Scope list for your models: it helps your stakeholders keep in mind what's out of scope and allows you to capture those items and either make the list available to a subsequent project or include the list with your project deliverables.

[4] This is a paraphrase of the quote frequently attributed to Albert Einstein, "Make everything as simple as possible, but not simpler."

or recognize. While the author recommends that a few of the diagram elements and icons included in this book <u>not</u> be used for requirements analysis purposes, they are included so that if you ever come across them in diagrams created by software designers or developers, you'll recognize and understand them.

UML keywords are a general mechanism that enables using the same diagram icon for multiple purposes and provides an extensibility feature that allows users to extend the language for their own purposes. In diagrams, they should be included within guillemets (e.g., «keyword»). They can be used on most UML icons. For example, the UML specification uses the general association notation (of a dashed arrow) to also indicate the "Include" relationship between two Use Case icons with the addition of the "Include" keyword. See `Figure 5-1 vehicle registration, UML Use Case diagram: system use case`, for sample use of the "Include" keyword. `Table A-1 UML Keywords Used in Business Analysis` lists the UML keywords that are appropriate for business analysis.

Any of the UML diagram types may optionally be enclosed in an icon known as a frame, represented by a rectangle with an embedded rectangle in the upper left corner with its bottom right corner cutoff that optionally contains a frame heading.

**Table 3-1 UML Frame Kinds**

| Frame kind name | Frame kind abbreviation | UML Diagram Types |
|---|---|---|
| **activity** | act | Activity |
| **class** | class | Class |
| **component** | cmp | Component |
| **composite structure** | | Composite Structure |
| **deployment** | dep | Deployment |
| **interaction** | sd | Communication, Interaction Overview, Sequence, Timing |
| **object** | | Object |
| **package** | pkg | Package |
| **state machine** | stm | State Machine |
| **use case** | uc | Use Case |

The frame heading may contain either the frame kind name (e.g., use case) or frame kind abbreviation (e.g., uc) followed by the diagram name (e.g., Vehicle Registration for a frame representing a Use Case diagram named Vehicle Registration). In this book, all diagrams are included in frames, which display the frame kind abbreviation (except for Deployment, Composite Structure, and Object diagrams, which display the frame kind name). For example, in `Figure 5-1 vehicle registration, UML Use Case diagram: system use case`, the frame heading indicates the diagram is a Use Case diagram (via the frame kind abbreviation of uc) and the diagram name is *vehicle registration*.

## Diagram Tips

- Use a set of consistent layout and appearance conventions (e.g., font, color, left-to-right or top-to-bottom organization, and page orientation of portrait or landscape) for each diagram type, as much as feasible. Try to maintain these conventions across the different diagram types.
- If the diagram will ever be used as a standalone artifact, or will ever be viewed by itself (i.e. outside of the document it's embedded in), include a consistent set of information in a UML Note icon (essentially a comment) in a standard location (e.g., top left corner, top middle) of each diagram:
  - the name of the system under analysis
  - the name of the diagram
  - the UML diagram type
  - the perspective of the model (e.g., business, system)
  - whether it is a model of the current (as is) or future (to be) system or business
  - the last update date and the creator's name or initials.

Including this information helps to clarify the intention of the diagram for the reader and frequently avoids confusion. For example, the UML Note icon in `Figure 3-1 UML Note` would be placed on a diagram for the Somestate Dept of Motor Vehicles, on a Use Case diagram named Motor Vehicle Registration System, that is of the system perspective, of the future system, and was last updated on October 20, 2011 by a person with the initials ND. A UML Note icon can be included in any of the UML diagram types, and it may be attached to most of the icons in a diagram. Thus they are an excellent tool to add explanatory text to any diagram. In this book, a UML Note icon has <u>not</u> been included in all the diagrams in order to conserve space. To compensate for that, the figure name for each diagram in the book includes the name of the diagram and its UML diagram type.

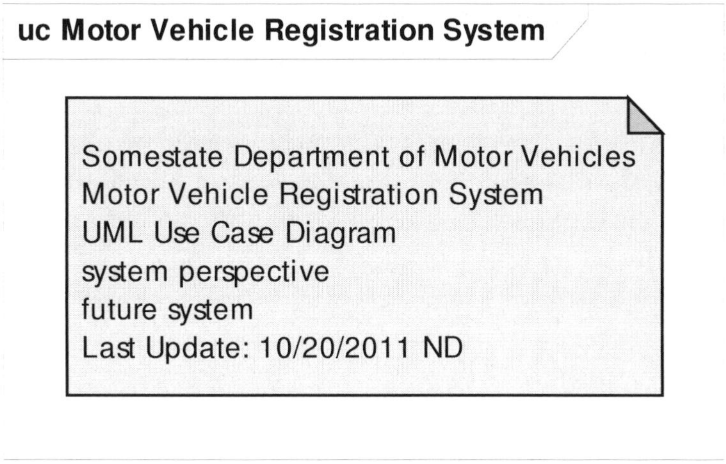

uc **Motor Vehicle Registration System**

Somestate Department of Motor Vehicles
Motor Vehicle Registration System
UML Use Case Diagram
system perspective
future system
Last Update: 10/20/2011 ND

**Figure 3-1 UML Note example**

- Keep diagrams to a manageable size. Too many items in a diagram may make it confusing for your readers.
- For diagrams, there is always a tradeoff between the amount of information to include and the time needed to understand the diagram. The more items on a diagram, the more time it takes to understand it. The fewer items in a diagram, the less information it conveys.
- Always keep in mind the purpose of your model. If the purpose is to convey high-level concepts to a target audience that is primarily interested in an overview, include only enough detail to accomplish that goal. If the purpose is to convey a lot of information, your diagram will be denser, include more details, and take longer to review and understand. If you're using a UML modeling tool, there are typically options to display different levels of detail in a diagram. Thus you might display considerable detail in a diagram to one audience, and display less detail to a different audience from the same model.
- Use the appropriate tools to assist in conveying the information. These include the usage of UML Note icons, UML keywords, and color coding.

## *How-to-Model Tips*

- It is typically preferable to address breadth first, then depth. For example, when creating a Class diagram, begin with the most important classes capturing just the class name, then add the associations between the classes, and finally, add the attributes with their details. This leads to overview results quicker than a depth-then-breadth approach.

- While a diagram will provide an excellent overview that readers can understand quickly, the associated text will generally fill in the important details.
- Remember, a diagram does not a model make! Most diagrams require all the associated text to make them clear, understandable, and complete. For example, Class models require high quality definitions for all the classes and attributes, and Use Case models require all the use case text to provide the details of a use case. It's best to capture the text detail after the diagram has been drafted, since the text detail generally takes the most time and effort.

## *Naming Guidelines*

- Use a set of consistent names across diagrams and models. This practice will provide clarity and help enhance the understanding of the diagrams and models.
- Use full names, not abbreviations or acronyms.
- Use lower case for most items. Exceptions include using initial upper case for proper nouns (e.g., actual system names, organization names) and optionally, diagram names.

Throughout the book, diagram and model examples are presented for a fictitious Somestate Department of Motor Vehicles. The Somestate Department of Motor Vehicles is a state government department that issues and manages driver's licenses, motor vehicle registrations, and motor vehicle titles for the state within a country.

All motor vehicles principally garaged within the state must have a valid motor vehicle registration in order to be driven on public roads. The cost for a motor vehicle registration for two years depends on the type of motor vehicle (e.g., automobiles $50, trucks $60, buses $80). The motor vehicle registrations are valid for a period of two years and must be renewed prior to the expiration date of the motor vehicle registration or the motor vehicle registration automatically expires. In order to be issued or renew a motor vehicle registration, the motor vehicle owner must have no unpaid parking fines[5].

In order to register a motor vehicle, the motor vehicle must have a valid motor vehicle title issued by the Somestate Department of Motor Vehicles. The motor vehicle title is a certification of ownership and is intended to ensure that stolen vehicles are not registered.

Driver's licenses are issued by the Somestate Department of Motor Vehicles to legal residents of the state after they pass both a written test and a road test that verifies their driving ability.

### Somestate Department of Motor Vehicles Glossary

The following is a sample portion of the organization's glossary.

- Department: An organizational unit of the state government.
- Dept: An abbreviation for Department.
- Driver's license: The legal authorization for a person to drive a motor vehicle granted by the Somestate Department of Motor Vehicles.

---

[5] A parking fine is an amount of money levied against a motor vehicle owner as a penalty for violating a parking regulation.

- Motor vehicle registration: A certification that the motor vehicle registration has been issued by the Somestate Dept of Motor Vehicles for a motor vehicle garaged in a city in the state.
- Vehicle owner: The person or organization that owns a motor vehicle.
- Vehicle title: The legal certification of ownership granted by the Somestate Department of Motor Vehicles to the owner of a motor vehicle.
- License Plate Number: A unique identifier for a motor vehicle registration in the state; it is displayed on the license plate.
- Registration Expiration Date: The date on which a motor vehicle registration status is scheduled to change from active to expired.

### *Somestate Department of Motor Vehicles Business Rules*[6]

The following is a sample portion of the organization's business rules.

- A motor vehicle registration is valid for a period of two years from the date it is issued or renewed.
- Motor vehicle registrations and renewals are allowed only if the motor vehicle owner has no unpaid parking fines.
- Motor vehicle registration renewals are allowed beginning three months before the expiration date.
- Motor vehicle registration reinstatements are allowed only if the motor vehicle owner has no unpaid parking fines.
- A motor vehicle registration is automatically expired when its expiration date is reached.
- A person must be a resident of the state to be issued a driver's license.
- A person must be at least sixteen years of age to be issued a driver's license.
- A valid vehicle title is required to register a motor vehicle.

---

[6] Business rules are worthy of an entire book. For further information on business rules, see [Ross, 2010], [von Halle, 2002], [von Halle, 2009].

Use Case models show both the events the system or business perform, as well as the people roles, systems, and devices (all three of which are referred to as actors) that participate in those events.

Use cases are one of the techniques included in the BABOK Version 2.0.

## *Purpose*

The most typical purpose of a Use Case model is to document the functional requirements of a proposed software system.

Use Case diagrams illustrate the boundary of the business or system as well as its responsibilities, and thus are a good tool to document the scope of a system.

Use case text describes the sequence of steps between the system and its various actors, including people actors, devices, and other systems.

Be aware that there are three distinct categories of Use Case models, each with a different focus:

- System: Use cases whose focus is a software system. Typically, the primary actor is attempting to achieve a goal utilizing the software system. In this case, the purpose of the Use Case model is to document the functional requirements of the software system. This is the most frequently used category. See `Figure 5-1 vehicle registration, UML Use Case diagram: system use case` for an example.
- Business: Use cases whose focus is the business processes of an organization, irrespective of any software systems. These use cases typically involves actors outside of the business (e.g., customer, supplier) interacting with the business to achieve their goal. See `Figure 5-2 Somestate Dept of Motor Vehicles System, UML Use Case diagram: business use case` for an example.
- Component: Use cases whose focus is a single component of a software system. These may be used to document the requirements for a particular software component. The actors are typically other software components of the system under analysis or external systems. This is the least frequently

used category. See `Figure 5-3 messaging component, UML Use Case diagram: component use case` for an example.

Each of the three categories of Use Case models can be used to document either an existing or a proposed system (or business or component).

## Guidelines

Start of rant: Under no circumstances should you ever utilize the term "use case" as a substitute for "reason" or "rationale" or "story". That is a travesty, and it dilutes the use of the term "use case". People do this quite frequently, but you needn't cave in to the crowd mentality. End of rant!

Remember, not everything is a use case!

Each Use Case diagram should be for just one of the categories: system, business, component. Avoid mixing the categories into a single Use Case model (i.e. when creating a business Use Case diagram, don't include component Use Case icons in it). Each category has a different scope, focus, and purpose.

Why are Use Case models so valuable?

- They allow each stakeholder to review only the portion of the model of concern to them.
- They allow anyone to receive a high level overview of a system in two minutes by reviewing the Use Case diagrams of interest.
- They allow anyone to delve deeper into the details of any use case simply by reading the text for a single use case.
- They allow for the appropriate level of review of each use case: high level, normal course, and exception conditions.

Use Case models are <u>not</u> as appropriate for:

- Documenting all non-functional requirements (although a use case is a good container for documenting non-functional requirements that are specific to that use case)
- Reporting applications, unless you utilize a technique[7] where business category use cases capture the decisions and actions the actors take based

---

[7] This technique was described to me by Susan Burk of EGB Consulting, Inc.

on the information in the report, and serve as a springboard to capture the detailed data requirements needed to support those decisions and actions

- Data requirements for data warehousing, unless you utilize a technique[8] where business category use cases capture the decisions and actions the actors take based on the information in the report, and serve as a springboard to capture the detailed data requirements needed to support those decisions and actions
- User interface design.

A Use Case model does not include all the requirements. While it is an excellent tool for documenting functional requirements, it's not well suited as the sole method for documenting all the non-functional requirements of a system. Non-functional requirements typically span multiple use cases. When non-functional requirements are included in the use case text representation, those are typically only the non-functional requirements specific to the use case in question. Use cases typically don't include the details of external interfaces, or data details.

A Use Case model consists of <u>both</u> the Use Case diagram(s) and the associated use case text for each use case. A Use Case diagram is a superb tool that provides stakeholders with a high-level overview of the model at a glance and allows them to quickly review it for completeness and scope. The use case text complements the diagram and is an excellent tool for providing the necessary details: the goal of the use case, the actors, the triggering event, the main success scenario, all the extension conditions, and the desired outcome. Both the diagram and the text have a critical use and place in a Use Case model.

For detailed guidance on Use Case modeling, see [Cockburn, 2001] and [Schneider et al., 2001].

### *Diagram Notation*

Become familiar with the following diagram elements for this diagram type. An example of most diagram elements is included in the first diagram of the Diagram Example section of this chapter. When that's not the case, the last row for that diagram element, labeled "Diagram examples", either includes one or more references to diagrams that contain that diagram element.

---

[8] This technique was described to me by Susan Burk of EGB Consulting, Inc.

## *Actor (frequently referred to as a stick figure)*

uc

actor name

| Informal definition | Generally, represents the role of a person or an external system or device that interacts with the system. |
|---|---|
| Used in diagrams | Use Case |
| Suggestions for use | Use to represent an external system, device, or role of a person that interacts with the system. While user-defined icons are allowed, typically don't use them in business analysis: there's no reason to confuse your readers by using multiple icons for the same purpose. For business category use cases, while not included in the UML specifications, a special business Actor icon is sometimes used; it includes a diagonal line through the bottom right portion of the icon's head. |

## *Use Case*

uc

use case name

| Informal definition | A diagram icon representing the series of steps (specified in the associated text representation of a use case) that take place between the associated actor(s) and the system under analysis to deliver value to the primary actor. |
|---|---|
| Used in diagrams | Use Case |
| Suggestions for use | Use to represent the series of steps that take place between the associated actor(s) and the system under analysis. For business category use cases, while not included in the UML specifications, a special business Use Case icon is sometimes used; it includes a diagonal line through the bottom right portion of the icon. |

The following icons fit into the **Diagram connectors** category:

## *Association*

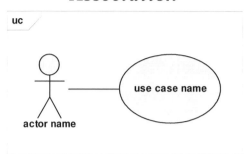

**(just the line between the two Use Case icons)**

| Informal definition | A general relationship between two diagram nodes, in this case between an Actor icon and a Use Case icon, indicating that the Actor participates in the performance of the Use Case. |
| --- | --- |
| Used in diagrams | Class; Deployment; Use Case |
| Suggestions for use | Use this to indicate an Actor that participates in the performance of the use case. See the Diagram Tips section of this chapter for a discussion of arrowhead usage. |

## *Extend*

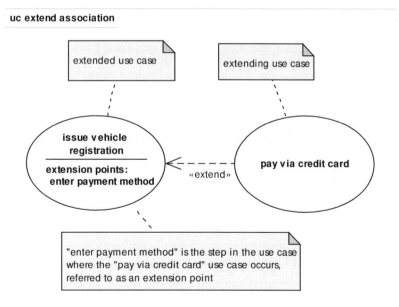

**(just the line between the two Use Case icons)**

| Informal definition | Extend represents a relationship between an optional use case (referred to the extending use case) and another use case for which the extending use case provides optional functionality (referred to as the extended use case). The open arrowhead points from the extending Use Case icon to the extended Use Case icon. |
|---|---|
| Used in diagrams | Use Case |
| Suggestions for use | Avoid using Extend relationships: you can just place the steps of the extending use case in the extended case (see the Extensions section of the Use Case Text Example in this chapter for examples of how to do that), and there's no reason to force your readers to learn an unnecessary diagram notation. The exception to avoiding Extend is if you "freeze" a set of use cases (i.e. don't allow any changes to them after they've been implemented), and then place all the use case steps and requirements for a future release in extending use cases (so that the requirements for the future release are explicitly separated in different use cases from those use cases already implemented). |
| Diagram examples | none |

## *Generalization*

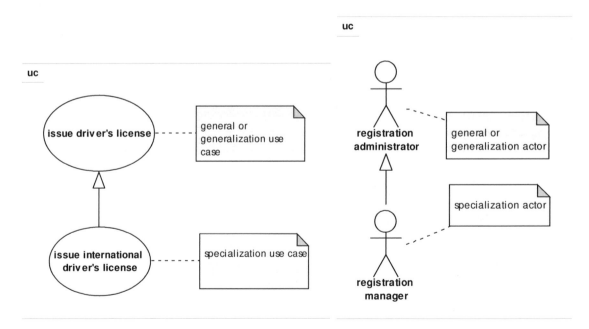

**(just the line between the two Use Case icons and the line between the two Actor icons)**

| Informal definition | For use cases, a relationship between two use cases where the one the triangle points to is the general Use Case and the one on the other end of the line is a special type of (also known as a specialization) the general Use Case. The special type of the general use case contains all of the main success scenario steps of the general use case plus additional main success scenario steps that are specific to that special type. For actors, a relationship between two actors where the one the triangle points to is the general Actor and the one on the other end of the line is a special type of the general actor that participates in all the use cases the general actor can plus additional use cases that are specific to that special type. |
|---|---|
| Used in diagrams | Class, Use Case |
| Suggestions for use | Use when appropriate. Multiple use cases that contain most of the same main success scenario steps but some steps that are specific can be modeled with a generalization use case and multiple specialization use cases. For example, if the use case "issue international driver's license" contains all of the steps that "issue a regular driver's license" does plus additional steps, model them as two use cases with a generalization relationship between the two, the triangle pointing to the "issue regular driver's license" (it being the general use case), indicating that "issue international driver's license" contains all of the main success scenario steps that "issue regular driver's license" does, plus additional main success scenario steps. Keep in mind that this adds another diagram icon that your readers will need to understand. |

## *Include*

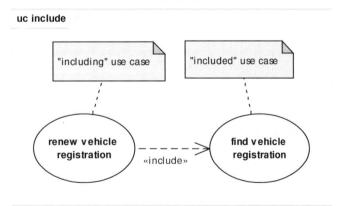

**(just the line between the two Use Case icons)**

| Informal definition | Include is a relationship that indicates the use case on the arrow side of the relationship ("included" use case) is logically a part of the use case from which the relationship extends ("including" use case). |
|---|---|
| Used in diagrams | Use Case |
| Suggestions for use | Use when you have a series of steps that accomplish a goal and that occur in multiple use cases. Remove the common series of steps and place them into their own "included" use case. Removing that series of steps from each of those use cases makes the use case text of each of them smaller, removes the redundancy, reduces maintenance time when there are changes to those common steps, and emphasizes to your readers that they are common. |

## Diagram Examples

Figure 5-1 vehicle registration, UML Use Case diagram: system use case, a system perspective UML Use Case diagram, indicates that a *registration administrator* initiates the *issue vehicle registration* use case, and also initiates the use case *renew vehicle registration* use case.

The *Wecolekt Credit Card Processing System* and the *Somestate Court System* are also involved in those two use cases. The *Vehicle Title System* is also involved in the use case *issue vehicle registration*. Both the *renew vehicle registration* and *revoke vehicle registration* include the *find vehicle registration* use case. The use case *expire vehicle registration* is initiated by *"time"* (while not illustrated in the diagram, the use case text would explain that the use case is initiated daily at 12:01am by the system itself, with no outside intervention). A *registration manager* can perform all of the same use cases as the *registration administrator* (as indicated by the Generalization relationship icon from the *registration manager* to the *registration administrator*), as well as the *revoke vehicle registration* use case.

The inner rectangle enclosing the Use Case icons represents the boundary of the system and highlights the fact that the Actors are outside the system.

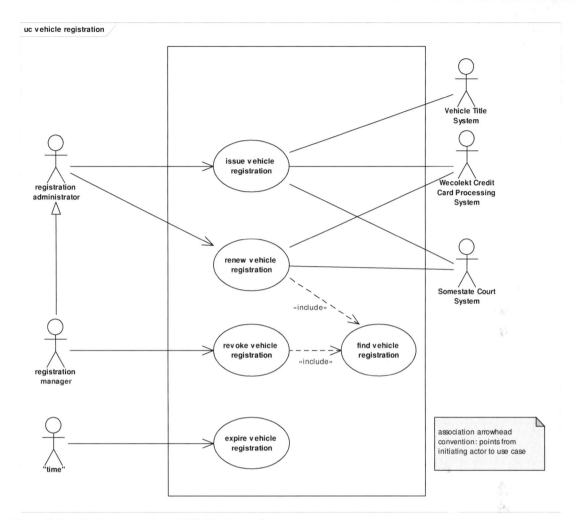

**Figure 5-1 vehicle registration, UML Use Case diagram: system use case**

Figure 5-2 Somestate Dept of Motor Vehicles System, UML Use Case diagram: business use case, a business perspective Use Case diagram, indicates that the *vehicle owner* initiates both the *issue vehicle registration* and the *renew vehicle registration* use cases, and that the *Somestate Court System* and the *Wecolekt Credit Card Processing System* are both involved in those use cases.

The *vehicle owner* is involved in the *send vehicle registration renewal reminder* use case, but does not initiate it (because there is no arrowhead pointing to the Use Case icon); the reader can conclude that the business initiates that use case. Similarly, *Driver's Licenses 'R Us* is involved in the *order driver's license card* use case, but does not initiate it. *Somestate Community Bank* is involved in the *pay invoice* use case, but does not initiate it.

uc Dept of Motor Vehicles business use case

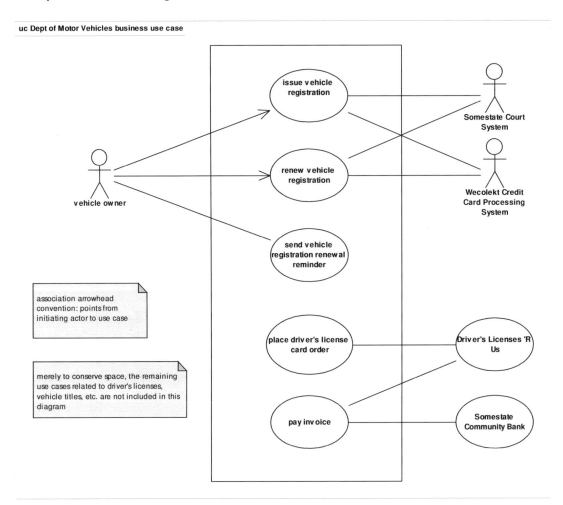

**Figure 5-2 Somestate Dept of Motor Vehicles System, UML Use Case diagram: business use case**

The inner rectangle enclosing the Use Case icons represents the boundary of the business and highlights the fact that the Actors are outside the business.

Figure 5-3 messaging component, UML Use Case diagram: component use case, a system perspective use case, indicates that either the *Somestate Vehicle Registration component* or the *Somestate Driver's License component* can initiate the *send unpaid parking fines balance inquiry* use case, in which the *Somestate Court System* also participates. Either the *Somestate Vehicle Registration component* or the *Somestate Driver's License component* can initiate the *send payment request* use case, in which the *Wecolekt Credit Card Processing System* also participates.

The inner rectangle enclosing the Use Case icons represents the boundary of the Somestate Messaging component and highlights the fact that the Actors are outside the component.

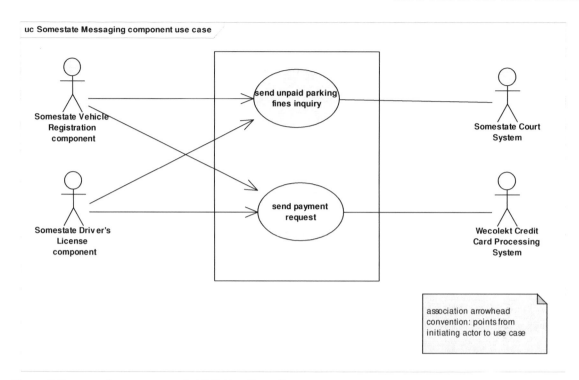

uc Somestate Messaging component use case

Somestate Vehicle Registration component

Somestate Driver's License component

send unpaid parking fines inquiry

send payment request

Somestate Court System

Wecolekt Credit Card Processing System

association arrowhead convention: points from initiating actor to use case

**Figure 5-3 messaging component, UML Use Case diagram: component use case**

## *Diagram Tips*

- Use a consistent diagram layout convention throughout all Use Case diagrams. Whenever feasible, place Use Case icons in the middle, initiating Actor icons on the left, secondary Actor icons on the right. This convention makes it easy for your readers to read and understand the diagrams.
- There is no time sequence between use cases implied in a Use Case diagram. However, invariably readers find it helpful if you sequence Use Case icons in the diagram either in a fashion that mimics the normal process flow or by state or workflow dependency. That's why the recommendation is to place your Use Case icons in order, typically with time or lifecycle progressing as you move down the page, and with all other aspects being equal, the use cases that are executed less frequently, lower in the diagram. For example, in Figure 5-1 vehicle registration, UML Use Case diagram: system use case *issue vehicle registration* is listed first (in the lifecycle of a vehicle registration, this use case needs to occur before any of the others in the Use Case diagram), followed by *renew vehicle registration* (the use case that occurs

most frequently and must follow *issue vehicle registration* in the lifecycle), and finally, *revoke vehicle registration* and *expire vehicle registration,* because these last two occur less frequently than those listed above them in the Use Case diagram.

- Use of arrowheads on the association between an Actor icon and a Use Case icon has been a topic of considerable debate. Usage varies among organizations and individual practitioners. Adopt one convention, document it, and use it consistently. Here are three common conventions:
    - use an arrowhead only to point from the initiating Actor icon to the Use Case icon. This is the author's recommendation because it's simple, easy to understand, visibly identifies the initiating actor, and doesn't clutter up the diagram with extraneous arrowheads
    - never use arrowheads
    - use arrowheads only when the communication is one-way.

- Avoid using arrowheads to always illustrate the direction of information flow because information flow is typically two way and this just results in a lot of arrowheads that tend to clutter the diagram. If you insist on showing the direction of information flow, use the last option from the preceding list instead because that results in the same amount of information and a less cluttered diagram. Activity diagrams, Sequence diagrams, or even Communication diagrams are more appropriate for illustrating the flow of information than a Use Case diagram.

- When using generalization relationships, place the general Use Case icon above the specialization Use Case icon(s) whenever possible, not below. Similarly, place the general Actor icon above the specialization Actor icon(s) whenever possible, not below it.

- When using Includes relationships, place the "included" Use Case icon either below or next to the "including" Use Case icon, not above.

## *Use Case Template*

There are numerous use case templates. Following are the descriptions of the sections of the use case template utilized in the Use Case Text Example in this chapter.

### USE CASE TEXT TEMPLATE (WITH INSTRUCTIONS)

**Use Case Name**: The brief name of the use case; used in the Use Case diagram.

**Use Case Category**: A categorization of what the use case applies to: system (the use case models the behavior of actors interacting with the software system), business (the use case models the interactions with the business), component (the use case models the requirements of a software component to other software components).

**Goal**: A brief one sentence description of what the primary actor is attempting to accomplish.

**Primary Actor**: The party or system that wishes to accomplish the goal of the use case. This is typically also the actor that initiates the use case.

**Secondary Actor(s)**: A list of the actors, other than the primary actor identified above.

**Brief Description**: A short (no more than one paragraph) description of the use case.

**Stakeholders and their Interests**: A list of stakeholders and their particular interests in the use case. To identify the stakeholders, think of all the people who will directly interact with the system, all the people and organizations that will provide information to or receive information from the system, and any others having an influence on or interest in the outcome.

**Trigger**: The action that begins the use case. Typically this is the initiating actor taking the first step (e.g., customer inserts card into slot in ATM machine), a predetermined point in time (e.g., end of day, month end), or a state-change (e.g., when an insurance policy expires).

**Precondition(s)**: For system use cases, these are conditions that the system must ensure are true before allowing the use case to begin (e.g., the user has been authenticated to the system).

**Post Conditions on Success**: These are the conditions that will be true when the use case completes successfully (e.g., the motor vehicle registration expiration date is two years in the future).

**Main Success Scenario**: This is the list of steps when everything goes right, sometimes referred to as the "sunny day" scenario or "happy path" or "basic path".

**Channel to Primary Actor**: Identifies the method used by the primary actor to communicate with the system (e.g., web browser, mobile phone, PDA).

**Extensions**: An alternative action that an actor or the system could take for the related use case step. An extension consists of the condition that was detected (e.g., an error condition the system detects such as "date of birth in the future" or "invalid license plate number") followed by the sequence of use case steps that then follow the occurrence of that condition and lead to the resolution, successful or unsuccessful, of the condition. Instead of the term extension, some use different terms depending on whether the use case steps end in success (sometimes called alternate success situation or alternate flow or alternate path) or failure (sometimes called exception or failure situation).

**Business Rules**: These identify the business rules that should be enforced by the use case. While a centralized business rules repository is the ultimate goal, documenting business rules within use case text may be utilized.

**Business Priority**: This indicates the relative priority (e.g., low, medium, high) to the business, typically as determined by the business sponsor or their delegate. This can be used to determine in which iteration the use case will be developed, if the project is using an iterative approach.

**Software Development Level of Difficulty**: The relative degree of difficulty in developing the use case as determined by the software development team. This can be used to help determining in which iteration the use case will be developed if the project is using an iterative approach.

**Frequency of Occurrence**: The expected frequency of usage (e.g., once per month; 2000 per weekday, 100 per non-weekday; 20 per second). This can be helpful in risk assessment, and then used in determining in which iteration the use case will be developed if the project is using an iterative approach, selecting high risk uses cases for early iterations.

**Release**: This identifies the system release in which the use case will be included (e.g., initial, next, later, or 1.0, 1.1, etc.) if the project will be implemented in distinct software releases.

**Status**: This indicates the workflow status of the use case (e.g., not begun, initial draft, approved, software development in progress, in production).

**Revision Number (or Date)**: This provides an indication of the currency of the use case text. This may be used in lieu of a requirements management system, document management system, or other configuration management system for requirements.

**Creation Date**: The date the use case was initially written.

**Last Revision Date**: The date the use case was most recently revised.

**Author**: The name of the person(s) who wrote the use case.

**Critical Reviewers**: The list of stakeholders who should review the use case.

**Open Issues**: A list of outstanding questions or issues about this use case. This may be used if there is no issue tracking system for the project.

## Use Case Text Example[9]

**Use Case Name**: renew vehicle registration

**Use Case Category**: System

**Goal**: Renew the owner's motor vehicle registration

**Primary Actor**: registration administrator (as proxy for vehicle owner)

**Secondary Actor(s)**: credit card processing system; state court system

**Brief Description**: The registration administrator provides motor vehicle identifying information and payment information, the system records the payment, renews the registration, and prints the new motor vehicle registration and payment receipt

**Stakeholders and their Interests**: vehicle owner - renew motor vehicle registration; registration manager - ensure all business rules are enforced, ensure appropriate payments are received

**Precondition(s)**: registration administrator has been authenticated to the system

**Post Conditions on Success**: owner has an active motor vehicle registration with expiration date two years in the future and a payment receipt, the Somestate Dept of Motor Vehicles has received the appropriate payment amount

**Channel to Primary Actor**: web browser

---

[9] Horizontal lines are included between sections of this example merely to delineate the different sections of the use case in the book.

**Main Success Scenario:**

The use case begins when the registration administrator requests motor vehicle registration renewal.

1.  The system requests entry of the license plate number.
2.  The registration administrator provides the motor vehicle license plate number.
3.  The system locates the motor vehicle registration information and the vehicle owner information.
4.  The system checks that the motor vehicle registration status is active and its expiration date is within the next three months. (BR115)[10]
5.  The system requests that the Somestate Court System provide the vehicle owner's unpaid parking fines.
6.  The state court system returns the vehicle owner's unpaid parking fines.
7.  The system returns the current status and expiration date of the motor vehicle registration, the name and address of the vehicle's owner, and the vehicle owner's unpaid parking fines.
8.  The registration administrator verifies that the vehicle owner's address on file is correct.
9.  The registration administrator enters the payment method (cash, check, credit card).
10. The system records the payment method, renews the motor vehicle registration and updates the expiration date to two years in the future (BR102).
11. The system prints the new motor vehicle registration.
12. The system prints the payment receipt.

The use case ends.

Steps 11-12 can occur in any order.

---

[10] This is one notation convention to identify a business rule, placing the business rule identifier in parenthesis immediately after the use case step where the business rule is to be enforced. See the Business Rules section of this use case text that follows the Extensions section of this example.

**Extensions:**

6.a. unpaid parking fines (BR110):

6.a.1. The system presents a message to the registration administrator indicating that the motor vehicle registration cannot be renewed because the vehicle owner has unpaid parking fines.

The use case ends.

10.a. payment via credit card:

10.a.1. The system requests entry of credit card information.

10.a.2. The registration administrator provides the credit card information.

10.a.3. The system sends a payment request message to the credit card processing system.

10.a.4. The credit card system debits the account of the credit card, credits the registry's account, and sends a response message to the registry system.

The use case continues at step 11.

10.a.4.a. credit card payment not accepted:

10.a.4.a.1 The system returns a message, the vehicle owner or their proxy is given the option to pay by another payment method and the use case continues at step 9.

---

**Business Rules[11]:**

BR102: Motor vehicle registrations are renewed for a period of two years

BR110: Motor vehicle registration renewals are not allowed if the vehicle owner has unpaid parking fines

---

[11] Susan Burk recommends this use of a Business Rules portion of a use case text template as the place for documenting the business rules (using their identifiers and names) enforced in the use case [Burk, 2004]. To avoid duplication, the text portion should be moved to a single business rules list. The text is included in this example for the convenience of the reader.

BR115: Motor vehicle registration renewals can begin no earlier than three months prior to the expiration date.

---

**Use Case Document Properties:**

The following items would typically be maintained as properties of a use case document in a requirements repository. They would only be included within the text of a use case if not maintained in a requirements repository.

**Business Priority**: high

**Software Development Level of Difficulty**: medium

**Frequency of Occurrence**: 4000 per day

**Release**: initial

**Status**: software development in progress

**Revision Number**: 2

**Creation Date**: 6/12/2011

**Last Revision Date**: 8/12/2011

**Author**: Bart Archibauld

**Critical Reviewers**: Raisa Renaut, Registration Manager; Ron Rosen, Lead Registration Administrator

**Open Issues**: none

## *Use Case Text Formats*

There are various formats for writing the steps of the text portion of use cases. If your organization has not decided on one, select one and use it consistently.

The following are two typical formats.

**Full sentences format**, typically beginning with the name of the actor and followed by the action(s) taken by that actor. For example:

- The system locates the motor vehicle registration information and the motor vehicle owner information
- The system requests that the state court system provide the vehicle owner's unpaid parking fines
- The state court system returns the vehicle owner's unpaid parking fines

**Table format**, with the actor name in one column, followed by the action(s) taken in the following column. For example:

| Actor Name | Action |
|---|---|
| system | locates the motor vehicle registration information and locates the vehicle owner information |
| system | requests that the Somestate Court System provide the vehicle owner's unpaid parking fines |
| state court system | returns the vehicle owner's unpaid parking fines |

Irrespective of the selected format option, you also have the option to allow either a single action or multiple actions within a single step.

| *One action within a single step:* | *Multiple actions within a single step:* |
|---|---|
| *The following example includes four steps, each step containing a single action.* | *The following example includes two steps, the first step containing three actions, the second step containing one action.* |
| <ul><li>*The system locates the motor vehicle registration information.*</li><li>*The system locates the vehicle owner information.*</li><li>*The system requests that the Somestate Court System provide the vehicle owner's unpaid parking fines.*</li><li>*The state court system returns the vehicle owner's unpaid parking fines.*</li></ul> | <ul><li>*The system locates the motor vehicle registration information, locates the vehicle owner information, and then requests that requests that the Somestate Court System provide the vehicle owner's unpaid parking fines.*</li><li>*The state court system returns the vehicle owner's unpaid parking fines.*</li></ul> |

There are advantages and disadvantages to each of these options.

Restricting a step to a single action highlights the individual actions and allows the extensions to be associated with the individual actions, but makes the use case text longer. Testers prefer this option because they can easily associate test cases with each single action.

Allowing a single step to include multiple actions makes the use case text smaller and groups together all the actions taken by an actor. But, it may result in creating many extensions for a single step and require a more involved method of linking the extensions and test cases back to the particular action within the step.

Again, select one option and use it consistently within a Use Case model.

Similarly, with all of the preceding options, you can number the steps or not. Numbering the steps makes it easy to discuss them and reference them from alternative paths. However, renumbering can be a challenge because all references to a step number must be changed, as well.

### How-to-Model Tips

- Always utilize an experienced use case facilitator. They will provide guidance to those unfamiliar with use case modeling, make certain your use cases are written at the appropriate level of detail, referee arguments over usage of "Include" and "Extend" relationships, etc. Failure to utilize an experienced use case facilitator is one of the top reasons for use case modeling failure.

- Always provide at least one high quality example Use Case diagram and associated use case text. Make certain the example follows all the conventions you have chosen. This helps immensely to avoid frustration and confusion for both business analysts as well as stakeholders. Optimally, have one example from outside your industry (so that your readers focus on understanding the example rather than focusing on whether or not it's perfect), and one example from within your organization. You want your stakeholders to see a high quality example of what you'll be creating for their project. If you're lucky, your stakeholders can identify use cases and write portions of the use case text; at a minimum they'll understand what you'll be creating for the project and will be good reviewers of your Use Case model.

- Always use a standard use case template for the text portion of a use case. Make it as easy to use as possible. Don't include all of the instructions in that use case template. You may, however, have a separate version of the template with all of the instructions included, so that those unfamiliar with the template can read this version. The Use Case Template section of this chapter contains a use case template with all of the instructions included.

- Avoid having software developers write use cases, it's an almost surefire way to allow design to creep into the requirements analysis process. However, be certain to have them review the use case text extensions and their resolution. This best utilizes their highly developed expertise in being able to identify exception conditions. Plus they should review the entire use case text, since they need to make certain it contains the necessary and sufficient information for designing and developing the software that implements the use cases.
- Similarly, make certain quality assurance personnel review the use cases. They are adept at identifying exception conditions and any portions that are not clear or not testable.
- Don't allow user interface detail to creep into use case text. The following phrases typically indicate that user interface specifications have invaded your use case text: click, checkbox, drop-down list, menu bar, mouse over, radio button, select from list. Those are part of user interface design.
- In the beginning, avoid spending a significant amount of time (i.e., more than two minutes) deciding whether to use Include or Extend associations, and whether to use a generalization relationship between actors or uses cases. Instead, wait until after the steps of the main success scenario and extensions have been written for the use cases. The best choice frequently becomes obvious at that point in time.

How do you know when a Use Case model is complete? When it satisfies all of the following conditions:

- The stakeholders agree that if the system provides the functionality specified in the use cases, it will meet their needs.
- The software development team agrees they have enough information to design and build the system.
- The testing team agrees they will be able to test the use cases.

## USE CASE STEPS

- Always write the steps in the main success scenario to end successfully.
- Typical step types in a use case include:
  - The system requesting the actor to provide data

- o The actor providing data to the system
- o The system validating data (typically after receiving the data from an actor)
- o The system performing a calculation
- o The system presenting the result to the actor
- o The system retrieving data from another actor
- o The system storing the data it received from the actor
- The initial step of a use case is typically taken by the initiating actor. Exceptions to that can be in those use cases triggered by time, where the system takes the initial step.
- The final step of a system category use case is always taken by the system.

The following are documentation conventions. If your organization has adopted any of these, follow them. If your organization hasn't adopted any of these, decide whether or not you're going to use any of them, then use them consistently.

- Some use the term "trigger" for the first step in the main success scenario. Some use the format "The use case begins when …" for the first step in the main success scenario.
- Similarly, in the main success scenario and in applicable extensions, some use "The use case ends" as the final step or preface the final step with "The use case ends when …". Some use "The use case terminates" or "The use case terminates unsuccessfully" as the final step in scenarios where the goal is not achieved.

### REPETITION OF STEPS

To indicate repetition, utilize one of the following two methods:

- <actor> does <something> until <some condition is satisfied>

For example, "The customer continues adding items to their shopping cart until they indicate they wish to proceed to pay".

- <actor> repeats steps m-n until <condition>

For example, "The customer repeats Steps 8 - 12 until they indicate they wish to proceed to pay."

### TIMING

To indicate timing, incorporate the following phrases:

- At any time between steps m and n, the user/actor will …
- As soon as the user has …, the system will …

To indicate that the order in which the steps occur is not relevant, incorporate the following phrase:

- Steps m-n can occur in any order

For example,

11. The system prints the new motor vehicle registration.
12. The system prints the payment receipt.

Steps 11-12 can occur in any order.

### EXTENSIONS

An extension is the condition detected and the series of use case steps that follows the detection of that condition, all specified separately in a portion of the use case text other than the main success scenario. This includes those extensions that may end in success (sometimes called alternate flows or alternate success situations) and those that may end in failure (sometimes called exceptions or failure situations). Each extension includes a condition that triggers the alternate flow, followed by a sequence of use case steps. For example, in the *renew vehicle registration* use case described in the Use Case Text Example section of this chapter, 6.a. *unpaid parking fines*, 10.a. *payment via credit card*, and 10.a.4.a. *credit card payment not accepted* are extensions.

- If you're numbering use case steps, identify the extension conditions with letters.

For example, for use case step number 2, the first extension is a, and the first step in that extension is number 1. Thus,

2a1. <Actor><action>

- Write the condition that was detected for the extension (e.g., time limit exceeded awaiting entry of thirty seconds; account number entry time-out), followed by a colon.

For example:

3a. unpaid parking fines:

5b. credit card payment not accepted:

- When there are multiple conditions associated with a given step, there is no sequence implied within letters, thus 2a and 2b identify two different conditions with two different paths for step 2, not a sequence of steps or conditions.
- For those extension conditions that can occur at any step, list them with no number, but prefix them with an asterisk and place them either before or after other extensions. For example,
- *b. At any time, the customer can choose to abandon shopping.
- Frequently, the final step of an extension is to return to a step in the main success scenario.

Here are some typical extension resolution categories:

- The condition is handled successfully; the step is successful
- The system allows the actor to retry
- The extension ends in failure
- There is a different path to success

## ACTORS

Identifying the actors in a Use Case model is important for several reasons:

- To identify the system users to elicit and review the requirements
- To identify all the people and systems that will need to interact with the system
- To assist in identifying the characteristics of the people who will utilize the system
- To identify the people who will require training
- To identify the people and systems that will require authorization to use the system

Some use cases are triggered based on time (e.g., weekdays at midnight, month-end close). There are several ways to deal with these situations:

- Create an Actor icon named "time", as in `Figure 5-1 vehicle registration, UML Use Case diagram`. Place the word "time" within quotes so that readers can easily distinguish it from people and system Actor icons.

- Create one Actor icon for each specific time (e.g., weekday midnight, month end). Place these actor names within quotes so that readers can easily distinguish them from people and system actors.
- Use no initiating Actor icon. Avoid this option because readers can easily confuse this with a Use Case for which the actor hasn't yet been identified.

Sometimes the person or organization with the goal that the use case fulfills does not interact with the system directly and thus isn't an actor. That regularly occurs when the actor is performing the data entry functions and thus can be considered a proxy for the person or system with the goal. In our example, the vehicle owner has the goal of obtaining a motor vehicle registration in the use case issue motor vehicle registration. However the vehicle owner does not interact with the system, the registration administrator does. In this case, describe the primary actor as "registration administrator (as proxy for vehicle owner)" or simply "registration administrator for vehicle owner".

## USE CASE GRANULARITY

One of the most difficult challenges for new use case modelers includes understanding and describing to their stakeholders the level of granularity that constitutes a good use case. Here are guidelines for system use cases:

- The actor goal is reasonable and one that subject matter experts would agree with.
- The five minute guideline: A system use case should take no more than five minutes to perform, from the initiation of the first step to the successful completion of the use case.
- The coffee break guideline: If you were an actor in a system use case, you wouldn't interrupt performing the use case to go on a coffee break. Pretend that you're at your desk performing a use case when a colleague stops by and says, "Will you join us for a coffee break?" You reply, "I'll meet you there as soon as I finish …" What you said after the word "finish" is a use case at the correct level (e.g., adding a new resource to the project plan, entering a purchase order, making a flight reservation, reserving a hotel room).
- The Goldilocks guideline: After enough experience, you'll become like Goldilocks of the children's story "Goldilocks and the Three Bears" when she tested the three beds, the three chairs, and the three bowls of porridge. When you read a use case, you'll immediately know whether "That use case is too high-level." (e.g., manage customer account), "That use case is

too small." (e.g., enter quantity), or, ideally, "That use case is just right!" (e.g., renew vehicle registration).

## *Naming Guidelines*

You may find that your junior high school grammar training really does help in naming the various aspects of Use Case models!

### ACTOR NAMES

- For actor names, use a singular noun or noun phrase (e.g., customer, purchaser, hotel guest).
- Actor names frequently end in "er" or "or" (e.g., customer, purchaser, registration administrator).
- Sometimes the business has no name for some of the actors. For example, subject matter experts may just think in terms of job titles (e.g., admitting clerk, assistant sales manager).
- When naming actors, avoid using organization-specific job titles. For example, avoid "senior director of operations" and use a term such as "store manager" instead; avoid "associate director of purchasing" and instead, use a term such as "purchasing agent".
- Avoid long debates (i.e. more than five minutes) about naming conventions for actors, particularly near the beginning of a project. Delay that decision until the vast majority of actors and use cases have been identified.
- Finalize actor names only after the vast majority of actors and use cases have been identified. At that time, you're typically able to see the big picture and identify the various use cases a given actor participates in. You can then make certain the actor is named the same in all the use cases in which they participate.
- Use role names that accurately reflect the actor's role in the business, for example "customer" or "reservation requestor". When that technique doesn't produce a high quality name, use a name that describes how they're participating in the use case. For example, "purchaser" describes how the actor is participating in the use case "purchase book from web site".
- When you can't come up with a good actor name, you can fall back on using a noun phrase derived from the verb portion of the use case name. For example, if the use case name is "issue motor vehicle registration", the actor name could be, "issuer of motor vehicle registration" or "motor vehicle registration issuer". While this method allows you to always come

up with an actor name, use this naming convention only if all other naming methods fail to produce a better actor name: this method results in actor names that frequently don't reflect a name that resonates with the business experts, results in a different actor name for each use case, and doesn't add substantial useful information to the Use Case model. Many actor names created using this method end in the letters "er" or "or" (e.g., a purchaser makes a purchase, a requester makes a request, an editor edits). Example actor names using this convention: claimant (makes a claim), purchaser (makes a purchase), and requester (makes a request).

## USE CASE NAMES

- Use case names consist of an active voice, present tense verb phrase, followed by a direct object phrase, most frequently in the singular (e.g., renew vehicle registration).
- Use business terms whenever feasible.
- Avoid use case names that include words such as "manage" and "perform". They're vague, typically do not resonate with the business experts, and are frequently indications of use cases at too high a level of granularity.
- Avoid technical terms in use cases. For example, "self-transition on active" is not a good choice for a use case name. Instead "change purchase order" or "update customer demographics" would be more appropriate.
- Think of how you'd respond to a question from a friend or colleague who noticed you having problems achieving your use case goal. Your response could be a good example of a use case. For example, if your colleague asked, "What are you trying to do?" you might respond, "Purchase a plane ticket".
- Examples of use case names: add task to project plan, apply for credit card, assign person to a project team, book flight reservation, cancel hotel reservation, change flight reservation, check flight status, evaluate credit risk, generate monthly invoice, pay for purchase, purchase airline ticket, request laboratory test, reserve rental car, schedule automotive service appointment, submit invoice, and withdraw cash from checking account.
- While it's tempting to think you could just assemble a list of "high quality" verbs to use when naming use cases, resist the temptation to force the use of your names. It's important that use case names resonate with your business stakeholders!

## USE CASE STEP VERBS

The following verbs for use case steps are both user interface and device independent:

- The actor <u>indicates</u> they wish to take some action.
- The actor <u>provides</u> some data.
- The actor <u>requests</u> a motor vehicle registration renewal.
- The actor <u>submits</u> the requested data.
- The system <u>assigns</u> a unique transaction identifier to the payment.
- The system <u>calculates</u> the total amount of the purchase.
- The system <u>confirms</u> the data provided is correct.
- The system <u>presents</u> some data to the actor.
- The system <u>requests</u> the actor provide some data.
- The system <u>stores</u> the data.
- The system <u>verifies</u> the provided data is valid.

For example, "the system verifies all the credit card information was supplied" instead of "the system checks to see if the credit card information was entered"; "the system requests the actor provide credit card information" instead of "the system prompts the actor for their credit card information".

## USE CASE EXTENSION NAMES

The extension condition is written as a phrase, not as a full sentence. Example conditions include "required data missing", "credit card expiration date in past", "data entry time limit exceeded".

The following are typical categories of conditions:

- An actor takes an unexpected action, where "unexpected" is just an action that is not the standard next step leading to success (e.g., cancel option selected)
- An actor takes no action (e.g., no user input after five minutes)
- The system discovers business rule violations when validating the data (missing credit card number, invalid state code)
- The system fails (e.g., system down, network connection unavailable)

## *Modeling Process Summary*

The following is both a general process you may use as well as the process used to create the Use Case model in the next section.

The "Compare with related UML diagrams and adjust as appropriate" item in the following list is written under the assumption that you are creating a comprehensive and detailed model including all the UML diagram types and that you wish to have concepts covered in multiple diagram types whenever applicable. Thus suggestions such as "Confirm that all of the Lifeline icons in Sequence and Communication diagrams are represented as Actor icons in the Use Case diagrams. Add any missing Actor icons." may not apply in your situation.

1. Identify the actors (e.g., *web site visitor, passenger, credit card processor).* Creating a quick draft of an actor list first helps stakeholders to think about who will be using the system. Then add external systems to the list. To identify actors, ask which groups of people and individuals directly interact with the system, which groups of people and individuals receive information from the system, what external systems need to obtain information from the system, and what external systems does the system need to obtain information from or interact with.

2. Discover the use cases (e.g., *view train line delay, view train line schedule, purchase train pass, add value to train pass, pay fare).* Create a list of the use case names, beginning with those most frequently performed, later expanding to the less frequently performed. You can use the actor list by asking what functions does the actor need the system to perform, what information do the external systems need from the system, when does the actor need to be notified of an event in the system, are there any external devices that need to interact with the system. Think about any administrative functions that may be needed (e.g., defining code sets, setting up username and passwords, authorizing access).

Some people reverse the above two steps, discovering use cases first then actors. That's strictly a process choice. However it's likely that after you get started you'll find yourself switching between the two (e.g., after identifying a new actor, you identify new use cases in which they participate, then identify additional new actors that also participate in those newly identified use cases). Be prepared to switch back and forth, that's natural.

If your team finds the above two steps difficult, you may be better off having your domain or subject matter experts describe or write a text narrative of the normal business process. Then you can extract the use case names and actors from that narrative.

3. Draw the Use Case diagram
   o Add the Use Case icons
   o Add the Actor icons
   o Associate the appropriate Actor icons to each Use Case icon

o   Add any generalization relationships and any appropriate UML Note icons (e.g., describing any association arrow conventions)

4. For each use case, write the primary actor's goal, a brief description of the use case, preconditions, post conditions on success, and identify all of the remaining actors. Writing the brief description of the use case should be relatively quick. Writing the goal of the actor may take a bit more time and thought.

5. For each use case, write the steps of the main success scenario. Think of this as the "sunny day" scenario where only good things happen. This takes more time than the previous step.

6. For each use case, identify the extension conditions (e.g., alternative actions an actor could take, error conditions the system detects such as date of birth in the future, or invalid license plate number). But at this time don't attempt to write the use case steps that occur after the system detects the extension condition.

7. For each use case, for each extension condition, write the use case steps that occur after the system detects the extension condition. These steps either result in the use case resuming at a step in the main success scenario, ending in failure of the actor achieving their goal, or achieving success by an alternate series of steps. Writing this portion takes a substantial amount of time and effort.

8. Go back and determine if there are any sequences of steps that are repeated in multiple use cases and if they should be extracted out to "Include" use cases and the diagrams updated.

The preceding "breadth first, then depth" approach provides progress quickly, deals with the easiest portions of writing use cases first, and reinforces learning by providing repeated practice on individual tasks.

Particularly if your team is not familiar with writing use cases, taking your most involved use case and attempting to write all of the detail of the main course steps, identifying all of the extensions as you write a main course step, and then resolving all of the alternative courses ("depth", all of the details of a single use case), would frustrate you and your stakeholder - progress would appear to be very slow, and since you are continually switching tasks, this process hinders immediate practice on newly acquired skills. That's why the "breadth first, then depth approach" is recommended.

9.  If the diagram will ever be viewed without its context information (current or future system, perspective, author, date created or last updated), add a UML Note icon similar to that in `Figure 3-1 UML Note`.

10. Compare the diagram with related UML diagrams and adjust as appropriate:

    o  Confirm that all of the Activities in the Activity diagrams are represented in a use case and add any missing use cases.

    o  Confirm that all of the Actions in the Activity diagrams are represented in either a use case name or in use case steps.

    o  Confirm that all of the Interaction Use icons and Interaction icons in the Interaction diagrams are represented as use cases (or steps in use cases). Add any missing use cases and use case steps.

    o  Confirm that all of the operations from the Class diagrams are represented as use cases or use case steps. Add any missing use cases and use case steps.

    o  Confirm that all trigger events from State Machine models are represented in either a use case name or steps within a use case. Add any missing use cases and use case steps.

    o  Confirm that all of the Lifeline icons in Sequence and Communication diagrams are represented as Actor icons in the Use Case diagrams. Add any missing Actor icons.

    o  Confirm that all of the communications represented by Message icons in Sequence and Communication diagrams are represented as use cases or use case steps. Add any missing use cases and use case steps.

    o  Confirm that all of the external entities in a Context diagram are represented by Actor icons in the Use Case diagrams. Add any missing Actor icons.

    12. Review and verify the model with the appropriate stakeholders.

## Case Study Example Diagram

Here is an example of how you might describe the following system perspective Use Case diagram to your stakeholders. A *web site visitor* initiates the *view train line schedule* use case, as well as the *view train line delay* use case. A *passenger* can initiate the *purchase train pass* use case and the *add value to train pass* use case, in both of which the *credit card processor* is also involved. A *passenger* can initiate the *pay fare* use case.

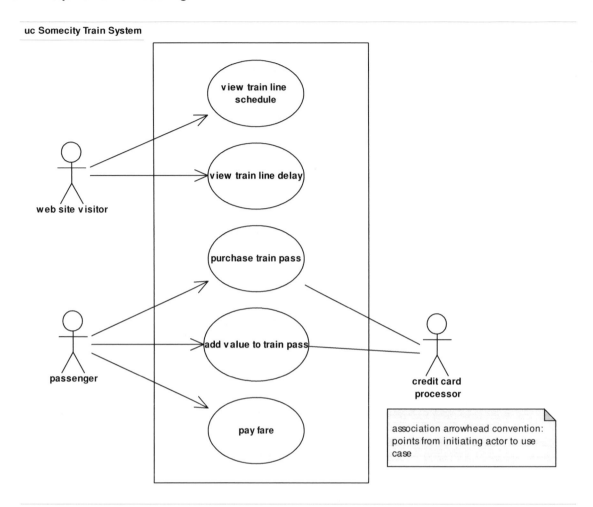

**Figure 5-4 case study, UML Use Case diagram, Somecity Train System: system use case**

## *Relationship to Other UML Diagrams*

- A use case may also be represented as an operation in a Class model, a trigger event in a State Machine model, an Activity diagram, or as one or more Activities and/or Actions in an Activity diagram.
- The steps of a use case may also be represented as an operation in a Class model, a trigger event in a State Machine model, one or more Activities or Actions in an Activity diagram, or as the communication represented by a Message icon in a Sequence or Communication diagram.
- An actor may also be represented as a Lifeline icon in a Sequence or Communication diagram.

Activity diagrams show the flow of actions and decisions in a business or system process, and the people roles and systems responsible for performing those actions.

Process modeling is one of the techniques included in the BABOK Version 2.0. UML Activity diagrams are one of the modeling notations mentioned, with flowcharts and Business Process Modeling Notation being the others.

## Purpose

Activity diagrams may be used by business analysts for many purposes:

- to model a business process
- to model workflow
- to depict the steps of a use case (e.g., one use case scenario, all possible scenarios) in diagram form
- to diagram a complex calculation
- to assist in identifying the data that needs to be passed between the different actions and actors in a business process or workflow, or steps in a use case

Activity diagrams may be used to document functional requirements.

Activity diagrams may be used by software designers and developers for other purposes, including modeling complicated logic or decisions.

## Guidelines

An Activity diagram may be at an overview level with minimal detail (e.g., `Figure 6-1 renew vehicle registration, UML Activity diagram, overview level`), at a detail level with considerable detail (e.g., `Figure 6-2 renew vehicle registration, UML Activity diagram, main success scenario`), or at any level in between.

Activity diagrams may be used to illustrate all of the possible scenarios of one use case, thus representing in diagram form the main success scenario and all of the use case extensions. Contrast the use of an Activity diagram to illustrate all of the

**55**

possible scenarios of one use case with the use of a Sequence diagram in Chapter 12 Sequence Diagrams to illustrate just a single use case scenario.

Use an Activity diagram to illustrate the workflow of a business or process.

Use an Activity diagram to visually illustrate decisions, branching, and the sequence of actions in a process.

Business Process Modeling (BPM) has become a popular term recently. The overlap between the Business Process Modeling Notation (BPMN) and Activity diagram notations is considerable. While there are differences, for the most part, one could use either. Select one notation and use it consistently, keeping in mind the biases of your organization and the tool support you have for the different notations.

## *Diagram Notation*

Become familiar with the following diagram elements for this diagram type. An example of most diagram elements is included in the first diagram of the Diagram Example section of this chapter. When that's not the case, the last row for that diagram element, labeled "Diagram examples", either includes one or more references to diagrams that contain that diagram element or indicates "none".

**Table 6-1 Activity Diagram Notation**

The following icons fit into the **Diagram nodes** category:

### *Accept Event Action*

act

| Informal definition | An icon indicating awaiting an event (typically from outside the process or diagram) or the passage of time. |
|---|---|
| Used in diagrams | Activity |
| Suggestions for use | Use this when the sender is not present in the same Activity diagram. A regular Action serves just as well when the sender is in the same Activity diagram. Compare the complementary Accept Event Action and Send Signal Action. |
| Diagram examples | none |

# *Action*

act

action name

| Informal definition | The most granular unit of behavior that can be represented in an Activity diagram. Contrast Action to Activity, which contains Actions or other Activities. |
|---|---|
| Used in diagrams | Activity |
| Suggestions for use | Use this to represent behavior that cannot be broken down further in an Activity diagram. Frequently people don't explicitly distinguish between Activity and Action and use them interchangeably. |

# *Activity Final*

act

⊙

| Informal definition | An ending point of an Activity diagram or Interaction Overview diagram. |
|---|---|
| Used in diagrams | Activity, Interaction Overview |
| Suggestions for use | Whenever it doesn't make the diagram layout difficult to read, use only one Activity Final icon on an Activity diagram. A single end point makes it easy for readers; they unconsciously recognize the commonalities of the multiple Actions that flow to the single Activity Final icon. Note that while Activity Final icon of an Activity diagram or Interaction Overview diagram and Final state icon of a State Machine diagram have the same visual appearance and serve analogous purposes, they represent different UML items. |

# *Data Store*

act

«datastore»
**datastore name**

| Informal definition | A representation of a persistent data repository (e.g., a database) that is referenced by multiple Actions. Sometimes referred to as "data at rest", it is the opposite of the Object Node icon for "data in motion". |
|---|---|
| Used in diagrams | Activity |
| Suggestions for use | Use when it's helpful to explicitly represent the persistent data that is indirectly exchanged between two Actions (e.g., by placing the data in a database that the sender writes to and the receiver or subsequent Action reads from), particularly when crossing Activity Partition boundaries. While it's allowable to create your own icons, avoid using icons other than the standard rectangle: there's no reason to confuse your readers. |
| Diagram examples | none |

## *Decision Node*

act

| Informal definition | This icon indicates that a decision must be made to take one of two or more alternate paths. |
|---|---|
| Used in diagrams | Activity, Interaction Overview |
| Suggestions for use | Use this to illustrate decisions resulting in alternate paths. Avoid placing Decision Node icons within the Activity Partition icons of external systems; see the Diagram Tips section of this chapter for the rationale. While they use the same icon, Decision Node icons can be distinguished from Merge Node icons because Decision Node icons have exactly one incoming flow and more than one outgoing flow, in contrast to Merge Node icons, which have more than one incoming flow and exactly one outgoing flow. |
| Diagram examples | Figure 6-6 prepare carrot cake, UML Activity diagram fragment, flow final node |

## *Flow Final*

act

| Informal definition | The end of an intermediary flow[12] but not the end of the Activity diagram or Interaction Overview diagram. |
|---|---|
| Used in diagrams | Activity, Interaction Overview |
| Suggestions for use | Use this to terminate an intermediary flow. Use when you have multiple occurrences of two or more consecutive Actions and some of the Actions in the multiple occurrences can proceed at the same time. This frequently occurs in assembly processes. |
| Diagram examples | `Figure 6-6 prepare carrot cake, UML Activity diagram fragment, flow final node` |

## *Fork Node*

act

| Informal definition | An icon specifying that the multiple outgoing flows can occur at the same time. |
|---|---|
| Used in diagrams | Activity, Interaction Overview |
| Suggestions for use | Use this to indicate the beginning of multiple activity flows that can occur concurrently. A Join Node icon is frequently used after a Fork Node icon. While they utilize the same icon, Fork Nodes can be distinguished from Join Nodes because Fork Nodes have exactly one incoming flow and more than one outgoing flow, in contrast to Join Nodes, which have more than one incoming flow and exactly one outgoing flow. |
| Diagram examples | `Figure 6-2 renew vehicle registration, UML Activity diagram, main success scenario,` the Fork Node immediately below the *record payment* Action in the *Somestate Dept of Motor Vehicles System* Activity Partition. |

## *Initial Node*

act

●

| Informal definition | The starting point of an Activity diagram or Interaction Overview diagram. |
|---|---|

---

[12] An intermediary flow is a branch of an Activity diagram, the termination of which does not terminate the entire Activity diagram.

| Used in diagrams | Activity, Interaction Overview |
|---|---|
| Suggestions for use | Typically, there is one Initial Node icon on an Activity diagram. Note that while the Initial Node icon of an Activity diagram or Interaction Overview diagram and Initial Pseudostate icon of a State Machine diagram have the same visual appearance and serve analogous purposes, they represent different UML items. |

## *Join Node*

act

| Informal definition | An icon indicating the completion of all incoming flows. |
|---|---|
| Used in diagrams | Activity, Interaction Overview |
| Suggestions for use | Use this to indicate that all incoming flows must be complete before the beginning of the next activity. A Join Node icon is frequently used after a Fork Node icon. While they utilize the same icon, Fork Nodes can be distinguished from Join Nodes because Fork Nodes have exactly one incoming flow and more than one outgoing flow, in contrast to Join Nodes, which have more than one incoming flow and exactly one outgoing flow. |
| Diagram examples | `Figure 6-2 renew vehicle registration, UML Activity diagram, main success scenario`, the Join Node below the *print receipt* and *print vehicle registration* Action nodes in the *Somestate Dept of Motor Vehicles System* Activity Partition. |

## *Merge Node*

act

| Informal definition | A point where different alternative paths, typically from a previous decision, come together. |
|---|---|
| Used in diagrams | Activity, Interaction Overview |

| Suggestions for use | Determine the extent to which you'll use these. Keep in mind that readers who are not familiar with the intricacies of the UML specifications frequently find the use of them confusing. See the final item in the Diagram Tips section of this chapter for an explanation and options. While they use the same icon, Merge Nodes can be distinguished from Decision Nodes because Merge Nodes have more than one incoming flow and exactly one outgoing flow, in contrast to Decision Nodes, which have exactly one incoming flow and more than one outgoing flow. |
|---|---|
| Diagram examples | Figure 6-8 merge node usage, UML Activity diagram fragment, correct usage of Merge and Action, the bottom most diamond icon. |

## *Object Node*

act

object name

| Informal definition | A representation of the specific information directly exchanged between two Actions or Activities. Sometimes referred to as "data in motion", it is the opposite of the Data Store icon used for "data at rest". |
|---|---|
| Used in diagrams | Activity |
| Suggestions for use | Use when it's helpful to explicitly represent and label the specific data that is directly exchanged between two Actions, or to explicitly represent documents and physical objects (e.g., receipts), particularly when crossing Activity Partition boundaries. While it's allowable to create your own icons, avoid using icons other than the standard rectangle to avoid confusing your readers. |
| Diagram examples | Figure 6-2 renew vehicle registration, UML Activity diagram, main success scenario, the *payment receipt* and *vehicle registration* icons near the bottom of the *registration administrator* Activity Partition. |

## *Send Signal Action*

act

send signal action name

| Informal definition | A representation of sending a notification or request. |
| --- | --- |
| Used in diagrams | Activity |
| Suggestions for use | Use this when the receiver of the message is not present in the same diagram. A regular Action serves just as well when the receiver is in the same Activity diagram. Compare the complementary Send Signal Action and Accept Event Action. |
| Diagram examples | none |

## *Time Event Action*

| Informal definition | A type of Accept Event Action that represents a time specification. |
| --- | --- |
| Used in diagrams | Activity |
| Suggestions for use | Use to indicate the beginning of a sequence of Actions based on time (e.g., end of month, midnight). Note that this icon need not have a Control Flow icon entering it. |
| Diagram examples | none |

The following icons fit into the **Diagram connectors** category:

## *Control Flow*

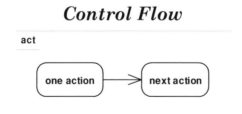

**(just the arrow between the *one action* Action and the *next action* Action icons)**

| Informal definition | A visual representation of the direction of the flow of control. |
| --- | --- |
| Used in diagrams | Activity, Interaction Overview |

| | |
|---|---|
| Suggestions for use | Use this to indicate the next item in the flow sequence. Note that while Control Flow icon of an Activity diagram or Interaction Overview diagram and Object Flow icon of an Activity diagram or Interaction Overview diagram have the same visual appearance and serve analogous purposes, they represent different UML items. |

## *Object Flow*

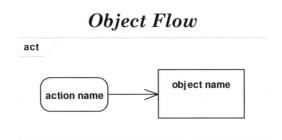

**(just the arrow from the Action icon to the Object icon)**

| | |
|---|---|
| Informal definition | Indicates the direction of the data movement. |
| Used in diagrams | Activity |
| Suggestions for use | Use this whenever you use an Object Node icon in an Activity diagram. An Object Flow can go either to or from an Object Node. Note that while Control Flow icon of an Activity diagram or Interaction Overview diagram and Object Flow icon of an Activity diagram or Interaction Overview diagram have the same visual appearance and serve analogous purposes, they represent different UML items. |
| Diagram examples | Figure 6-2 renew vehicle registration, UML Activity diagram, main success scenario, the arrow between the *print receipt* Action icon and the *payment receipt* Object Node icon. |

The following icons fit into the **Diagram containment** elements category:

## *Activity*

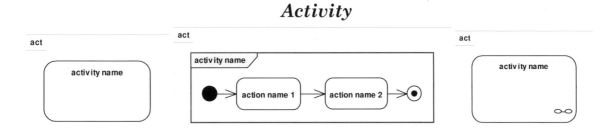

| | |
|---|---|
| Informal definition | A container for Actions or other Activities. |
| Used in diagrams | Activity, Interaction Overview |

| Suggestions for use | Use this to represent a sequence of Actions and/or other Activities. Contrast Activity with Action, which is the most granular level. The Activity icon may optionally include the diagram of the contained Activities or Actions, as the second diagram fragment above[13] does. The Activity icon may optionally include an "eyeglass" icon, as in the third diagram fragment above, to indicate that the Activity is a "composite" and that there is an Activity diagram associated with it; UML modeling tools typically allow the user to directly display that Activity diagram. |
|---|---|
| Diagram examples | Figure 6-3 typical workday, UML Activity diagram, containing activity, the *prepare for work* and *work* Activities. |

## Activity Partition *(informally known as swimlane or partition)*

act activity partition

| activity partition name |
|---|
| |

| Informal definition | A bounded portion of an Activity diagram used to segregate the group of Actions, Activities, Decisions, etc. performed by a single actor. |
|---|---|
| Used in diagrams | Activity |
| Suggestions for use | Use this whenever feasible to visually indicate the actor that's responsible for carrying out the Actions or Activities or making the Decisions. |
| Diagram examples | Figure 6-2 renew vehicle registration, UML Activity diagram, main success scenario, the *registration administrator*, *Somestate Dept of Motor Vehicles System*, and *Somestate Court System* Activity Partition icons |

---

[13] The tool used to generate that diagram fragment used the atypical rectangular frame icon rather than the normal Activity icon used in the other two diagram fragments.

## *Expansion Region*

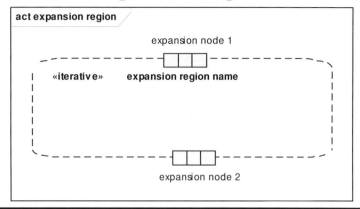

| Informal definition | A grouping mechanism that indicates that the enclosed Actions occur multiple times. |
|---|---|
| Used in diagrams | Activity |
| Suggestions for use | Use this to indicate the repetition of the enclosed items, such as when one action/activity produces multiple outputs and the outputs must all be processed by an intermediary process, also included in the Expansion Region, before the subsequent action/activity commences. Indicate the kind of execution with one of the expansion kind keywords: iterative, meaning the executions of the region must occur in sequence, one for each input; parallel, meaning the executions of the region may occur concurrently; stream, meaning the execution of the region occurs once, processing all of the inputs and producing the outputs all at once. |
| Diagram examples | Figure 6-5 book editing, UML Activity diagram fragment, expansion region |

## *Diagram Examples*

Figure 6-1 renew vehicle registration, UML Activity diagram, overview level, a system perspective UML Activity diagram, indicates that the first step in *renew vehicle registration* is *provide identifying information for current vehicle registration*, followed by *pay for vehicle registration renewal*, and concluding with *renew vehicle registration*.

This diagram represents an overview of the process represented by the use case *renew vehicle registration* from Figure 5-1 vehicle registration, UML Use Case diagram: system use case.

**Figure 6-1 renew vehicle registration, UML Activity diagram, overview level**

Figure 6-2 renew vehicle registration, UML Activity diagram, main success scenario, a system perspective Activity diagram, indicates that the successful renewal of a vehicle registration begins when a *registration administrator requests vehicle registration renewal.*

Then the system *requests identifying information,* and the *registration administrator provides identifying information.* Next the system *confirms the vehicle registration status,* then *requests the unpaid parking fines* from the *Somestate Court System.*

The *Somestate Court System provides the unpaid parking fines* (fortunately, there are none), followed by the system *requests payment information.* Then the *registration administrator provides payment information.* The system updates the *vehicle registration expiration date,* and then *records the payment.* The system *prints a receipt* and *prints a vehicle registration,* in any order. The process doesn't end until both the printing of the receipt and the printing of the vehicle registration have completed.

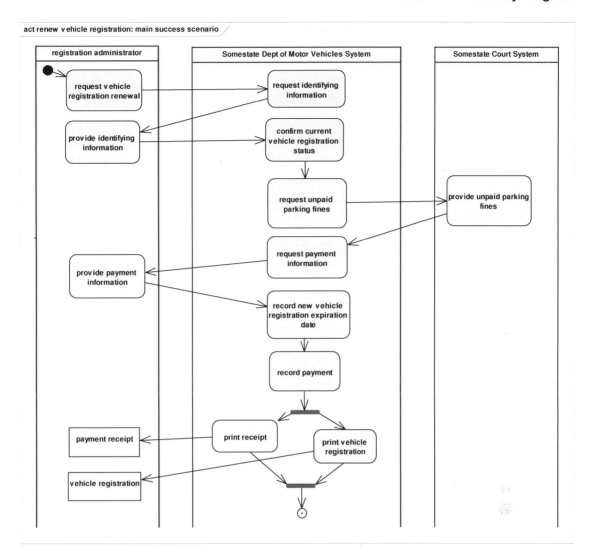

**Figure 6-2 renew vehicle registration, UML Activity diagram, main success scenario**

Note that this diagram is a representation of the process represented by the Use Case Text Example in Chapter 5 Use Case Models. Also, the lifeline names match the actor names in the Figure 5-1 vehicle registration, UML Use Case diagram: system use case.

Figure 6-3 typical workday, UML Activity diagram, containing activity, a business perspective UML Activity diagram, indicates that in a typical workday, a person *wakes up, prepares for work, travels to work, works, travels to home, eats dinner, relaxes,* and *goes to bed.* Both *prepare for work* and *work* are Activities: they contain either other Activities or Actions, as indicated by the small icon consisting of two connected ellipses in the bottom right corner of the Activity icon. The Actions and Activities those two Activities contain are not displayed in the diagram. Instead, each of the two Activities has its own Activity diagram.

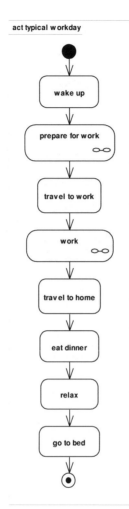

**Figure 6-3 typical workday, UML Activity diagram, containing activity**

Figure 6-4 prepare for work, UML Activity diagram, actions within an activity, a business perspective UML Activity diagram, indicates that within the *prepare for work* Activity, the following Actions occur in sequence: *shower*, *get dressed*, *make lunch*, *eat breakfast*, *brush teeth*.

Note that the diagram name *prepare for work* matches its parent Activity name in the previous diagram. While that's not required, avoid confusing your readers by using different names.

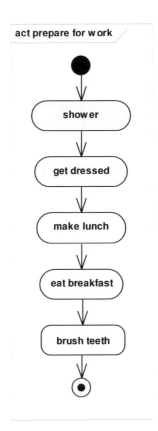

**Figure 6-4 prepare for work, UML Activity diagram, actions within an activity**

Figure 6-5 book editing, UML Activity diagram fragment, expansion region, a business perspective UML Activity diagram of a hypothetical book editing process, indicates that *assign editor for each of a book's chapters* occurs first, then, concurrently (as indicated by the UML keyword "parallel"), each editor *edits* their chapter, and only after all editors have finished can *return book to author with editor comments* occur. This illustrates the use of an Expansion Region.

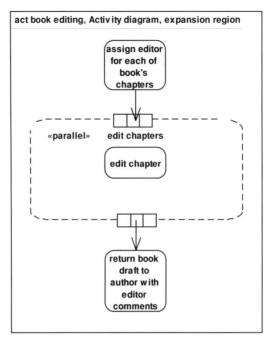

**Figure 6-5 book editing, UML Activity diagram fragment, expansion region**

Figure 6-6 prepare carrot cake, UML Activity diagram fragment, flow final node, a fragment of a business perspective Activity diagram to illustrate preparing a carrot cake, indicates that *peel carrot* occurs, then both (a) if there are *more carrots to peel, peel carrot* occurs again (until there are *no more carrots to peel*), and (b) *cut carrot* can occur concurrently.

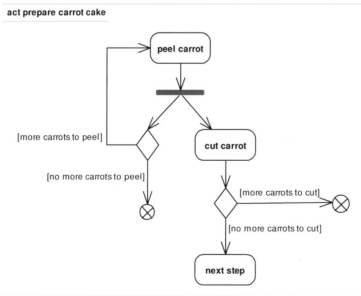

**Figure 6-6 prepare carrot cake, UML Activity diagram fragment, flow final node**

This portion of the process terminates when there are *no more carrots to cut*. This diagram illustrates the usage of the Flow Final icon, the open circle enclosing an "X", to terminate a flow but not terminate the entire Activity diagram.

## Diagram Tips

- Use Activity Partition icons whenever feasible to indicate the actors responsible for performing a group of Actions, Activities, Decisions, etc.

- Whenever possible, use a consistent diagram layout convention for all your Activity diagrams, e.g., time running top to bottom with the Activity Partitions running vertically (as they do in the examples in this chapter), or time running left to right with the Activity Partitions running horizontally.

- Sequence the Activity Partitions in the order in which they appear in the main success scenario of the process being modeled. If that results in too many Activity Partitions being crossed too many times, reorder the Activity Partitions to simplify the diagram by minimizing the number of lines crossing partitions.

- Always label the guard conditions, an expression that evaluates to either true or false and controls the flow, coming out of a decision point. See `Figure 6-6 prepare carrot cake, UML Activity diagram fragment, flow final node` for examples.

- It's typically best to label all of the guard conditions coming out of a decision point explicitly, so that your readers can ensure all of the conditions have been identified. However, there may be times when you need to simplify a diagram that has too many guard conditions coming out of a single decision, many having the same outbound flow. When it's unambiguous, you can consolidate some of the outbound flows into a single one and label its guard condition [else] or [otherwise]. For example, if you had a decision for payment method with only two outbound flows and one guard condition was labeled "credit card", the other could be labeled "else".

- Include guard conditions on Control Flow icons to illustrate the business rule(s) to be enforced before allowing the flow.

- Place the "normal" or most frequent sequence of actions in a straight line with the exceptions and alternate actions off to the side. This allows your readers to easily navigate through the normal course of actions, rather than getting distracted by all the possible courses of action.

- Activity diagrams can get complicated and large. One way to simplify them is to substitute an Activity icon for a portion of an Activity diagram.

UML software tools allow drilling down through the Activity icon to view its constituent Activities and Actions. See `Figure 6-3 typical workday, UML Activity diagram, containing activity` and `Figure 6-4 prepare for work, UML Activity diagram, actions within an activity` for an example of this.

- Avoid placing Decision Node icons in the Activity Partition icons of external systems. You shouldn't be concerned about the internal processing of external systems, only their information exchanges with the system under analysis. Instead, within the system under analysis Activity Partition icon include a Decision Node icon indicating how to handle the various responses from the external system. This keeps both the knowledge of and enforcement of business rules within the system under analysis.

- Decide how you will handle the use of Merge Nodes. The correct interpretation of UML Action icons will have an influence on this decision. The following discussion and two diagram fragments illustrate two options.

## MERGE NODE USAGE

Many people would interpret `Figure 6-7 merge node usage, UML Activity diagram fragment, incorrect usage of Action` to indicate that after the *previous action* occurs, either there is a request for help (in which case the *display help text* occurs) or there is not a request for help, but in <u>either</u> case, then the *next action* occurs.

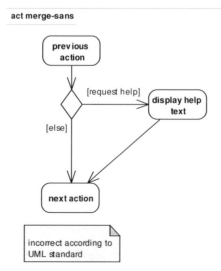

**Figure 6-7 merge node usage, UML Activity diagram fragment, incorrect usage of Action**

However, according to the UML specification, the correct interpretation is that *next action* can't occur until <u>both</u> the flow along the [*else*] path and the flow along the [*request help*] path occur, clearly a logical impossibility. This is because the official specification of the Action icon is that it does not execute until <u>all</u> incoming flows occur.

Figure 6-8 merge node usage, UML Activity diagram fragment, correct usage of Merge and Action has a Merge Node icon just before the *next action* Action icon. This Merge Node icon indicates that the outgoing flow to the *next action* Action icon can occur after either of the incoming flows into the Merge Node icon occurs.

You have two choices:

1. Follow the UML specifications and include Merge Node icons, as appropriate. You will almost certainly need to explain the use of the Merge Node icons to your readers. This also makes your Activity diagrams more involved, larger, and more challenging for most readers. This is a good choice if your Activity diagrams need to be precise and will be used as part of a specification for automating a workflow.
2. Don't follow the UML specifications and avoid the use of Merge Node icons in cases such as those illustrated in Figure 6-8 merge node usage, UML Activity diagram fragment, correct usage of Merge and Action.

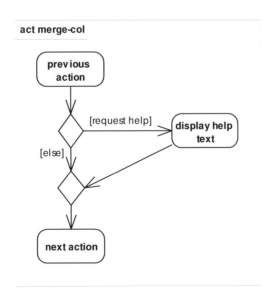

**Figure 6-8 merge node usage, UML Activity diagram fragment, correct usage of Merge and Action**

In this case, you should document your non-conforming usage and make clear to your readers that when two flows terminate on an Action icon it means that just <u>any</u> <u>one</u> of them need to occur. This is a good choice if your readers aren't familiar with the strict interpretation of UML for Action icons, or your Activity diagrams won't be used as specifications for automating a workflow.

## How-to-Model Tips

- Think of an Activity diagram as a diagram of a process, as a visual representation of an activity, or as a flow chart.
- It's generally easiest to outline the main series of actions, analogous to the main success scenario steps of a use case, then identify any decisions to be made, and then model the actions in the various outbound branches of the Decision Flow icons.
- If you will be using Activity Partition icons, first identify and name those that are needed, so that stakeholders get used to thinking about which of the actors is responsible for performing the activities as they identify the Actions/Activities.
- If your Activity diagram gets too large or complicated, use Activities to replace one or more series of Actions. This makes the diagram smaller and easier to read.

## Naming Guidelines

- Name Actions and Activities with an active voice verb in the present tense, followed by a direct object phrase (e.g., eat dinner, make offer, prepare for work, print receipt, provide identifying information, record payment, request vehicle registration renewal, sign sales agreement). The direct object phrase is generally in the singular. In cases where the next item is an Expansion Region, the direct object phrase will generally be in the plural.
- Name Object Node icons with a noun phrase, typically singular (e.g., payment receipt, sales agreement).
- Name the guard conditions on outgoing flows from a decision either with a noun phrase (e.g., cash, credit card), with a past participle (e.g., accepted, rejected) or with a clause that evaluates to true or false (e.g., unpaid parking fines).

- Name the Activity Partitions using a noun phrase in the singular form (e.g., registration administrator, Somestate Court System). Use actual system names, typically as proper nouns, whenever possible (e.g., Somestate Court System, Somestate Dept of Motor Vehicles System, and Wecolekt Credit Card Processing System). Use the same name as the name of the appropriate Actor in the corresponding Use Case diagram or external system in the Context diagram.

## *Modeling Process Summary*

The following is both a general process you may use as well as the process used to create the Activity diagram in the next section.

The "Compare with related UML diagrams and adjust as appropriate" item in the following list is written under the assumption that you are creating a comprehensive and detailed model including all the UML diagram types and that you wish to have concepts covered in multiple diagram types whenever applicable. Thus suggestions such as "Confirm that all of the Lifeline icons in Sequence and Communication diagrams are represented as Actor icons in the Use Case diagrams. Add any missing Actor icons." may not apply in your situation.

1. Identify the first step in the process.
2. List other typical steps in the process (where everything goes smoothly in the normal sequence of steps).
3. Identify the actors. They will be represented using Activity Partition icons in the diagram.
4. Identify the last step in the process.
5. Draw the initial diagram.
   o Add and name the Activity Partition icons.
   o Add the first, then the remaining Action icons and Activity icons in time sequence, but don't connect them with Control Flow icons yet.
6. Finish the diagram.
   o Identify any decision points, steps where something could go wrong, alternate actions, etc.
   o Add the Decision Node icons, identified in the previous step, and Control Node icons to the applicable Action icons or Activity icons, etc. and add any new Action/Activity icons needed. Add Merge Node icons, when needed, for the corresponding Decision Node icons.

- o Add any Object Node icons and their Object Flow icons where it's important to visually indicate the data being transferred between Actions or Activities or across Activity Partition icons.
- o Add any Data Store icons and their Object Flow icons where it's important to visually indicate that data is being exchanged via a database.
- o Add any remaining items, such as Fork and Join nodes, etc.

7. If the diagram will ever be viewed without its context information (current or future system, perspective, author, date created or last updated), add a UML Note icon similar to that in `Figure 3-1 UML Note`.

8. Compare with related UML diagrams and adjust as appropriate:
   - o Confirm that all of the use cases from the Use Case model are represented as Activity or Action icons. Add any missing Activity and Action icons.
   - o Confirm that use case extensions are represented as Decision icons in the Activity diagrams. Add any missing Decision Node icons.
   - o Check if any operations from the Class model are missing as Activity or Action icons. Add any missing Activities and Actions.
   - o Check if any trigger events from the State Machine models are missing as Activities or Actions. Add any missing Activities and Actions.
   - o Check if any Message icons from any Sequence diagrams or Communication diagrams should be added as Object Node icons. Add any Object Node icons, as appropriate.
   - o Check if any external entities from the Context diagram should be added as Activity Partition icons.

9. Review and verify the model with the appropriate stakeholders.

## *Case Study Example Diagram*

Here is an example of how you might describe the following system perspective UML Activity diagram to your stakeholders. The process *purchase train pass* begins when the *passenger* indicates that they wish to *purchase a train pass*. Then the *Somecity Train System presents the train pass amount choices*. Next, the *passenger indicates their amount choice*, and then the *Somecity Train System presents payment choices*. The *passenger indicates payment choice,* and then the *Somecity Train System presents payment instructions*. Next, the *passenger provides payment*. If the *payment choice is credit card*, the *Somecity Train System requests payment* from the *Trustuswequick credit card processor*. Then the *Trustuswequick credit card processor processes the payment.* Whether the payment choice was *cash* or *credit card,* the *Somecity Train System records the payment.* Then, possibly concurrently, the *Somecity Train System prints a payment receipt* and *issues train pass,* then *presents take pass instructions* to the *passenger.* Finally, the *Somecity Train System presents options for next transaction* and the use case process ends.

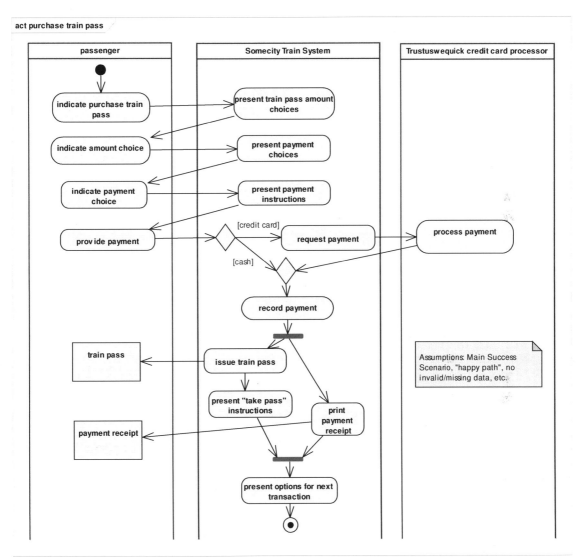

**Figure 6-9 case study, UML Activity diagram, purchase train pass**

## Relationship to Other UML Diagrams

- Actions and Activities may be represented by a use case or a series of steps in a use case, by an operation in a Class model, or by a trigger event in a State Machine model.
- Object Nodes may be represented by Messages in a Sequence or Communication diagram.
- Activity Partitions may be represented as Lifeline icons in Sequence or Communication diagrams and as external entities in a Context diagram.

Interaction Overview diagrams provide an overview of the control flow of a system or business process. They contain the overview actions and decisions involved in the process. Individual Actions are typically not included. Messages and Activity Partitions are not directly included, but may be illustrated in an embedded Sequence or Activity diagram.

Interaction Overview diagrams are one of the four diagram types in the UML Interaction diagram category.

Interaction Overview diagrams are not included in the BABOK Version 2.0 because they are used infrequently by business analysts.

## *Purpose*

Interaction Overview diagrams are functionally similar to Activity diagrams, but since they don't contain either Activity Partition or Message icons, they provide more of an overview and contain less detail than a corresponding Activity diagram would. They could be used instead of an Activity diagram when just an overview is desired, or to emphasize that certain activities involve interactions with other systems, which would then be modeled using a Sequence diagram embedded in the Interaction Overview diagram, which is confusingly referred to in UML as an Interaction.

Interaction Overview diagrams may be used by business analysts to illustrate an interaction flow at an overview level as a series of Interactions or Sequence diagrams.

They could also be used to create a summary of a use case flow when an Activity diagram would be too detailed.

## *Guidelines*

Interaction Overview diagrams will be used infrequently, if ever, for business analysis purposes. Use only when the alternatives of Activity and Sequence diagrams won't suffice, since Activity and Sequence diagrams will be more familiar to your readers than Interaction Overview diagrams. For example, if you need to visually illustrate multiple message exchanges between systems with multiple decisions and branches, a Sequence diagram is not a good fit and an Activity diagram may become too large; embedding Sequence diagrams in an Interaction Overview diagram using the Interaction icon is an alternative.

## *Diagram Notation*

Become familiar with the following diagram elements for this diagram type. An example of most diagram elements is included in the first diagram of the Diagram Example section of this chapter. When that's not the case, the last row for that diagram element, labeled "Diagram examples", either includes one or more references to diagrams that contain that diagram element or indicates "none".

**Table 7-1 Interaction Overview Diagram Notation**

The following icons fit into the **Diagram nodes** category:

## *Activity Final*

sd

| Informal definition | An ending point of an Activity diagram or Interaction Overview diagram. |
|---|---|
| Used in diagrams | Activity, Interaction Overview |
| Suggestions for use | Whenever it doesn't make the diagram layout difficult to read, use only one Activity Final on an Interaction Overview diagram. A single end point makes it easier or readers because they unconsciously recognize the commonalities of the multiple Actions that flow to a single Activity Final. Note that while Activity Final icon of an Activity diagram or Interaction Overview diagram and Final state of a State Machine diagram have the same visual appearance and serve analogous purposes, they represent different UML items. |

## *Decision Node*

sd

| Informal definition | This icon indicates that a decision must be made to take one of two or more alternate paths. |
|---|---|
| Used in diagrams | Activity, Interaction Overview |
| Suggestions for use | Use this to illustrate decisions resulting in alternate paths. While they use the same icon, Decision Node icons can be distinguished from Merge Node icons because Decision Nodes have exactly one incoming flow and more than one outgoing flow, in contrast to Merge Node icons, which have more than one incoming flow and exactly one outgoing flow. |

## *Flow Final*

sd

| Informal definition | The end of an intermediary flow, but not the end of the Activity diagram or Interaction Overview diagram. |
|---|---|
| Used in diagrams | Activity, Interaction Overview |
| Suggestions for use | Intermediary paths are seldom used in Interaction Overview diagrams. Use this to terminate an intermediary path. |
| Diagram examples | `Figure 6-6 prepare carrot cake, UML Activity diagram fragment, flow final node` |

## *Fork Node*

sd

| Informal definition | An icon specifying that the multiple outgoing flows can occur at the same time. |
|---|---|
| Used in diagrams | Activity, Interaction Overview |
| Suggestions for use | Use this to indicate the beginning of multiple activity flows that can occur concurrently. A Join Node icon is frequently used after a Fork Node icon. While they utilize the same icon, Fork Nodes can be distinguished from Join Nodes because Fork Nodes have exactly one incoming flow and more than one outgoing flow, in contrast to Join Nodes, which have more than one incoming flow and exactly one outgoing flow. |

| Diagram examples | Figure 6-2 renew vehicle registration, UML Activity diagram, main success scenario, the Fork Node immediately below the *record payment* Action in the *Somestate Dept of Motor Vehicles System* Activity Partition. |
|---|---|

## *Initial Node*

**sd**

| Informal definition | The starting point of an Activity diagram or Interaction Overview diagram. |
|---|---|
| Used in diagrams | Activity, Interaction Overview |
| Suggestions for use | Typically, there is one Initial Node icon on an Interaction Overview diagram. Note that while Initial Node icon of an Activity diagram or Interaction Overview diagram and Initial Pseudostate icon of a State Machine diagram have the same visual appearance and serve analogous purposes, they represent different UML items. |

## *Interaction*

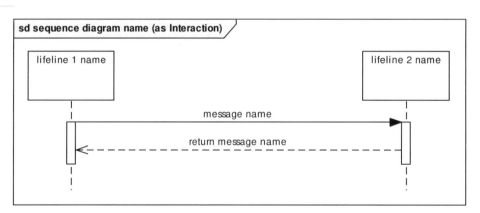

| Informal definition | An icon representing another diagram of the UML Interaction diagram category (Sequence, Communication, Timing, or Interaction Overview diagram) and including the icons of that referenced UML interaction category diagram. In the previous diagram fragment, the entire frame labeled "sd sequence diagram name (as Interaction)" is the Interaction |
|---|---|

| | |
|---|---|
| | (the frame contains a Sequence diagram).[14] |
| Used in diagrams | Interaction Overview, Sequence |
| Suggestions for use | Use this to represent an Interaction specified outside of this diagram and include the diagram of that interaction. Sequence diagrams are the type of Interaction most frequently used; Communication diagrams, Timing diagrams, and Interaction Overview diagrams may also be used. Contrast the Interaction Use and Interaction icons and note that Interaction icons contain more information on the diagram. Utilize an Interaction icon if you have diagram space and want to include more details than an Interaction Use icon allows. |
| Diagram examples | Figure 7-1 renew vehicle registration, UML Interaction Overview diagram, the *check unpaid parking fines* Interaction and the *successful vehicle registration renewal* Interaction. |

## *Interaction Use*

```
sd interaction use

┌─────────────────────────────────────────────┐
│ ref ╲                                         │
│      ╲          interaction use name          │
│                                               │
└─────────────────────────────────────────────┘
```

| | |
|---|---|
| Informal definition | An icon representing another diagram of the UML Interaction diagram category (Sequence, Communication, Timing, or Interaction Overview diagram). The name of the Interaction Use refers to the other diagram being represented. In the previous diagram fragment, the entire frame labeled "ref" is the Interaction Use. |
| Used in diagrams | Interaction Overview, Sequence |
| Suggestions for use | Utilize this to simplify an Interaction Overview diagram by including less detail, or to conserve space in an Interaction Overview diagram, or to factor out common behavior that can then be referenced (rather than duplicated) in other diagrams. Contrast the Interaction Use and Interaction icons and note that Interaction icons include more information on the diagram. |

---

[14] The notation for the Sequence diagram is covered in Chapter 12 Sequence Diagrams.

| Diagram examples | Figure 7-1 renew vehicle registration, UML Interaction Overview diagram, the *obtain vehicle registration and vehicle owner information* and *process payment* Interaction Use, and Figure 7-2 case study, UML Interaction Overview diagram, purchase train pass details, the *obtain train pass desired amount information, pay with cash,* and *issue train pass* Interaction Use icons. |
|---|---|

## *Join Node*

sd

| Informal definition | An icon indicating the completion of all incoming flows. |
|---|---|
| Used in diagrams | Activity, Interaction Overview |
| Suggestions for use | Use this to indicate that all incoming flows must complete before the beginning of the subsequent activity. A Join Node icon is frequently used after a Fork Node icon. While they utilize the same icon, Fork Nodes can be distinguished from Join Nodes because Fork Nodes have exactly one incoming flow and more than one outgoing flow, in contrast to Join Nodes, which have more than one incoming flow and exactly one outgoing flow. |
| Diagram examples | Figure 6-2 renew vehicle registration, UML Activity diagram, main success scenario, the Join Node below the *print receipt* and *print vehicle registration* Actions in the *Somestate Dept of Motor Vehicles System* Activity Partition. |

## *Merge Node*

sd

| Informal definition | A point where different alternative paths, typically from a previous decision, come together. |
|---|---|
| Used in diagrams | Activity, Interaction Overview |
| Suggestions for use | Determine the extent to which you'll use these. Keep in mind that readers who are not familiar with the intricacies of the UML specifications frequently find the use of them confusing. See the final item in the |

| | Diagram Tips section of Chapter 6 Activity Diagrams for an explanation and options. While they use the same icon, Merge Nodes can be distinguished from Decision Nodes because Merge Nodes have more than one incoming flow and exactly one outgoing flow, in contrast to Decision Nodes, which have exactly one incoming flow and more than one outgoing flow. |
|---|---|
| Diagram examples | Figure 6-8 merge node usage, UML Activity diagram fragment, correct usage of Merge and Action, the bottom most diamond icon. |

The following icons fit into the **Diagram connectors** category:

## *Control Flow*

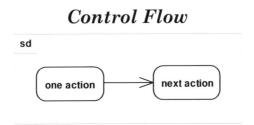

**(just the arrow between the one action Action and the next action Action icons)**

| Informal definition | A visual representation of the direction of flow. |
|---|---|
| Used in diagrams | Activity, Interaction Overview |
| Suggestions for use | Use this to indicate the next item in the flow sequence. Note that while Control Flow icon of an Activity diagram or Interaction Overview diagram and Object Flow icon of an Activity diagram or Interaction Overview diagram have the same visual appearance and serve analogous purposes, they represent different UML items. |

The following icons fit into the **Diagram containment elements** category:

## *Activity*

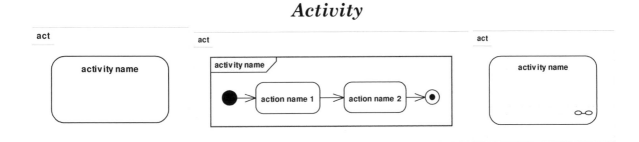

| Informal definition | A container for Actions or other Activities. |
|---|---|
| Used in diagrams | Activity, Interaction Overview |
| Suggestions for use | Although it is allowed and can be used as described in the following paragraph, the author recommends not using an Activity in an Interaction Overview for two reasons: to minimize the number of different icon types that your reader needs to recognize in the diagram, and to keep the diagram at an overview level. If more detail is needed, use an Activity diagram instead. Otherwise use an Interaction Use icon, or possibly an Interaction icon.<br><br>Use this to indicate an Activity that is broken down further into other Activities or Actions. Contrast Activity with Action, which is the most granular level. The Activity icon may optionally include the diagram of the contained Activities or Actions, as the second diagram fragment above[15] does. The Activity icon may optionally include an "eyeglass" icon, as in the third diagram fragment above, to indicate that the Activity is a "composite" and that there is an Activity diagram associated with the Activity; UML modeling tools typically allow the user to directly display that Activity diagram. |
| Diagram examples | Figure 6-3 typical workday, UML Activity diagram, containing activity, the *prepare for work* and *work* Activities. |

## Diagram Example

Figure 7-1 renew vehicle registration, UML Interaction Overview diagram, a system perspective UML Interaction Overview diagram, indicates that renew vehicle registration begins with *obtain vehicle registration and vehicle owner information* (an Interaction Use, just a reference to the Sequence diagram that illustrates that process is included), then *check unpaid parking fines* is performed (an Interaction, the Sequence diagram of that process is included).

---

[15] The tool used to produce that diagram fragment used the atypical rectangular frame icon rather than the normal Activity icon used in the other two diagram fragments.

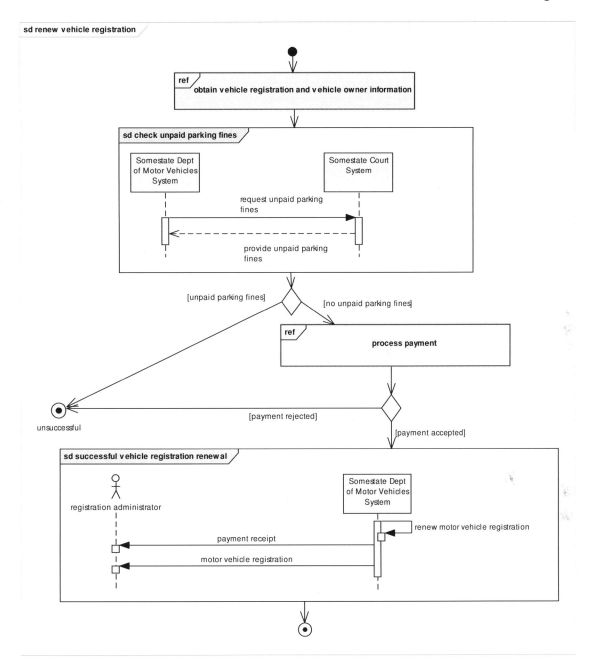

**Figure 7-1 renew vehicle registration, UML Interaction Overview diagram**

If there are *unpaid parking fines*, the process terminates unsuccessfully. If there are *no unpaid parking fines*, *process payment* occurs (an Interaction Use, just a reference to the Sequence diagram that illustrates that process is included). If the *payment is rejected*, the process terminates unsuccessfully. If the *payment is accepted*, the *successful vehicle registration renewal* process is performed (an Interaction, the

Sequence diagram of that process is included) and the *renew vehicle registration* process ends in success.

Note that this diagram represents an overview of the renew vehicle registration Use Case in `Figure 5-1 vehicle registration, UML Use Case diagram: system use case`, the Use Case Text Example in Chapter 5 Use Case Models, and `Figure 6-2 renew vehicle registration, UML Activity diagram, main success scenario`.

## Diagram Tips

- Most of the diagram tips for Activity diagrams and Sequence diagrams also apply to Interaction Overview diagrams.
- To have the entire embedded Sequence diagram displayed in the Interaction Overview diagram, utilize the Interaction Use icon. This could take up considerable space, but provides a significant amount of detail. *Check unpaid parking fines* and *successful vehicle registration renewal* in `Figure 7-1 renew vehicle registration, UML Interaction Overview diagram` are examples of this.
- To have just the title of the Sequence diagram viewable in the Interaction Overview diagram, utilize the Interaction Use icon, where just the Sequence diagram name is displayed rather than the entire Sequence diagram. This is useful for providing a high level overview or to save diagram space when the reader is familiar with the contents of the embedded Sequence diagram from its name. The *obtain vehicle registration and vehicle owner information* and *process payment* Interaction Use icons in `Figure 7-1 renew vehicle registration, UML Interaction Overview diagram` are examples of this.

## How-to-Model Tips

- Identify the high level major processes to be included in the diagram. Create the appropriate sub-diagram for each of the major processes. Typically, this would be a Sequence diagram, but could optionally be a Communication, Timing, or even another Interaction diagram. Determine if that sub-diagram will be referenced from (using an Interaction Use icon) or embedded into (using an Interaction icon) the Interaction Overview diagram.

- One way to think of an Interaction Overview diagram is as a summary or high level Activity diagram with embedded Sequence diagram(s) replacing a series of Activities or Actions.

## Naming Guidelines

- Diagram elements use the same naming conventions as the corresponding elements on an Activity diagram or Sequence diagram.
- Name frames of Interaction and Interaction Use with either with a verb phrase (e.g., check unpaid parking fines), similar to a use case name, or with a noun phrase (e.g., successful vehicle registration renewal).

## Modeling Process Summary

The following is both a general process you may use as well as the process used to create the Interaction Overview diagram in the next section.

The "Compare with related UML diagrams and adjust as appropriate" item in the following list is written under the assumption that you are creating a comprehensive and detailed model including all the UML diagram types and that you wish to have concepts covered in multiple diagram types whenever applicable. Thus suggestions such as "Confirm that all of the Lifeline icons in Sequence and Communication diagrams are represented as Actor icons in the Use Case diagrams. Add any missing Actor icons." may not apply in your situation.

1. Identify the high level major processes to be included in the diagram.
2. Determine which of those major processes should be displayed with their details (e.g., Sequence diagrams) as Interaction icons. Create those Sequence diagrams or other Interaction diagram types.
3. Determine which of those major processes should be displayed just as a reference utilizing an Interaction Use icon.
4. Draw the diagram.
   o Add all the Interaction and Interaction Use icons.
   o Add any needed Decision Node and Merge Node icons.
   o Add any needed Fork and Join Node icons, if needed.
   o Add all the associations (Control Flow icons).
5. If the diagram will ever be viewed without its context information (current or future system, perspective, author, date created or last updated), add a UML Note icon similar to that in Figure 3-1 UML Note.

6. Compare the model with related UML diagrams and adjust as appropriate:
   o Ensure the names match with the original Communication, Sequence, Timing, and Interaction Overview diagrams embedded utilizing Interaction icons or referenced utilizing Interaction Use icons.
7. Review and verify the model with the appropriate stakeholders.

## *Case Study Example Diagram*

Here is an example of how you might describe the following system perspective UML Interaction Overview diagram to your stakeholders.

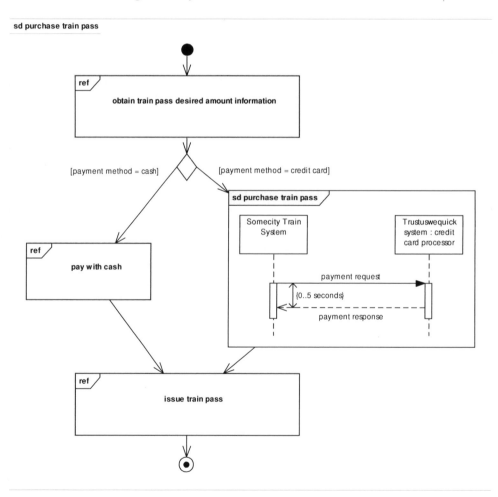

**Figure 7-2 case study, UML Interaction Overview diagram, purchase train pass details**

The *purchase train pass* process begins with *obtaining the train pass desired amount information*. Then, if the *payment method is cash*, the *pay with cash* process occurs. If the *payment method is credit card*, the *Somecity Train System* sends a *payment request* message to the *Trustuswequick credit card processor,* which replies within *five seconds* with a *payment response* message. Then the *issue train pass process* occurs, and the *purchase train pass* process ends.

## Relationship to Other UML Diagrams

- Interaction Overview diagrams can be used to illustrate a series of steps in a Use Case.
- At a higher level of granularity, Interaction Overview diagrams can be used to illustrate the sequential relationship of several Use Cases.
- Both an Interaction icon and an Interaction Use icon can represent a Sequence diagram (or a Communication, Timing, or another Interaction Overview diagram.

Class models show the significant business entities (e.g., persons, places, events, concepts) that are relevant to the system or business under analysis, the relationships those entities have to each other, the information the business needs to capture about them (referred to in UML Class Models as attributes), and the actions performed on the classes (referred to in UML Class Models as operations). Thus they create a holistic view of the system under analysis.

While object modelers and data modelers have different focuses and terminologies, fortunately for business analysis purposes, none of their disagreements affect your requirements modeling. Your primary goal is to produce a model of items important to the business for the project, not a software design or database design. Thus, this book treats Class models and data models as similar, with the exception that Class models contain operations. Your object modelers can use your Class model as the basis for their software design. Your data modelers can use your Class model as the basis for their database design. You've assisted each of them in understanding the items important to the business for the project.

Thus, when used for business analysis all of the guidelines and tips for data models also apply to Class models. Data models are treated separately in Chapter 19 Data Models Using Class Diagram Notation. Relevant material from that chapter is included in this chapter for the convenience of the reader.

While UML Class diagrams are included in the BABOK Version 2.0 as a modeling notation for data models, the BABOK does not include operations, and thus does not suggest Class diagrams as a tool for documenting the actions performed on the classes. The author finds the use of Class diagrams, including operations, to be valuable for several reasons:

- Class diagrams are helpful in presenting a single view of the system under analysis to both people who are process-oriented (the majority of business analysts), and people who are data-oriented (a minority of business analysts)[16]

- The identification of operations is helpful for user experience designers. The operations indicate the actions that will be performed on the class. The user interface will need to allow the user to perform those operations (e.g., with a menu option on a screen or web page that contains the attributes of the class).
- The tracing of operations to use cases can uncover missing use cases. The tracing of operations to state machines can uncover missing state transitions. The tracing of operations to Activity diagrams can uncover missing Action or Activity icons.

## *Purpose*

Class models may be used by business analysts to summarize both the data aspects and behavioral aspects of a system or business in a single model. The data aspects can be documented in detail using the attributes of a class. The behavioral aspects, the actions performed on the classes, can be documented at a higher level using the operations of a class.

Thus Class models may be used to document a portion of functional requirements of a system or business. This usage of Class models is the focus of this chapter.

Class models are used by software designers and developers to describe the interactions of the actual software classes in object oriented systems. For example, they might include a Window class with operations maximize, minimize, and set focus. These are at a distinctly different perspective from Class models created for business analysis purposes. Note that traditionally, Class diagrams have been used for this purpose and most of the examples you see in the typical software literature reflect this perspective. This usage of Class models is not covered in this book except to provide an example in `Figure 8-2 arguments, UML Class diagram fragment, software implementation perspective`.

---

[16] Informal surveys of more than a dozen different groups of approximately twenty business analysts each indicated that in each, approximately three fifths self-categorized themselves as process-oriented, one fifth as data-oriented, and one fifth as both.

## *Guidelines*

Keep the purpose of a Class model as described in the preceding section in mind. Also remember the Daoust Associates TAPS guideline defined in the Guidelines section of Chapter 3 General UML Diagram Guidelines:

- $\underline{T}$arget $\underline{A}$udience
- $\underline{P}$urpose
- $\underline{S}$cope

Just as with Use Case models, it's the text portion of the Class model that often takes the longest amount of time. Constructing good definitions for classes and attributes takes considerable practice. Malcolm Chisholm has an entire book devoted to definitions [Chisholm, 2010].

Table 8-3 Class Model Data Definitions, vehicle registration, partial text example lists the definitions of the classes and attributes of the associated Class diagram in Figure 8-1 vehicle registration, UML Class diagram.

## *Diagram Notation*

A Class icon can have three compartments, separated by horizontal lines. The top compartment contains the class name, the middle compartment contains the attributes of the class (the data elements), and the bottom compartment contains the operations of the class (the actions that can be performed on it). While the UML specifications allow for not displaying the attribute or operation compartments, leaving them out can be confusing to readers. Be consistent and always include all three compartments in Class diagrams.

The associations between two classes have multiplicities on either end. Those are represented as lower bound .. upper bound, where lower bound can be 0, 1, or any other integer, and upper bound can be 1, *, or any other integer. Thus the multiplicity of 0..1 indicates a minimum of zero and a maximum of 1. There are standard alternate conventions: just the number 1, indicating 1..1 (exactly one), and just a * indicating 0..* (a minimum of zero and no maximum). Keep in mind that your readers may not be familiar with these alternate conventions. The asterisk, "*", technically represents "unlimited"; however it is frequently read and interpreted as "many".

Attributes also have multiplicity. Options for specifying attribute multiplicity and a recommendation are included in the Diagram Tips section of this chapter.

Become familiar with the following diagram elements for this diagram type. An example of most diagram elements is included in the first diagram of the Diagram Example section of this chapter. When that's not the case, the last row for that diagram element, labeled "Diagram examples", either includes one or more references to diagrams that contain that diagram element or indicates "none".

**Table 8-1 Class Diagram Notation**

The following icons fit into the **Diagram nodes** category:

### *Class*

**class class**

| class name |
| --- |
| attribute name:  analysis datatype |
| operation name |

| | |
| --- | --- |
| Informal definition | An entity of importance to the business that also contains data elements and/or operations that are performed on it. |
| Used in diagrams | Class, Composite Structure |
| Suggestions for use | Use a Class icon in requirements to indicate real world items (e.g., people, organizations, places, things, events, and business transactions). In software design and software engineering, classes are frequently used to represent software artifacts (e.g., query window). |

The following icons fit into the **Diagram connectors** category:

### *Aggregation*

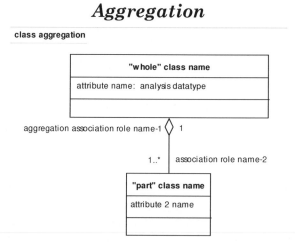

**class aggregation**

**(just the line between the two Class icons and its association role names and multiplicities)**

| Informal definition | A whole-part relationship, where the "whole" class is made up of or contains the "part" class. Aggregation can represent physical containment, a collection, or parts. The diamond is on the end of the whole/aggregate Class icon. |
|---|---|
| Used in diagrams | Class |
| Suggestions for use | Avoid the use of both aggregation and composition relationships for business analysis purposes: you don't need to use them, software developers may devote inordinate amounts of time arguing over whether an association should be aggregation or composition, you'll need to explain the icons to business stakeholders, business stakeholders will argue over whether an association should be aggregation or composition, and they add no useful information to business stakeholders that can't be represented using appropriate association role names (e.g., contained in, part of, composed of). They are included so that if you ever come across them in diagrams created by software designers or developers, you'll recognize and understand them. |
| Diagram examples | none |

## *Association*

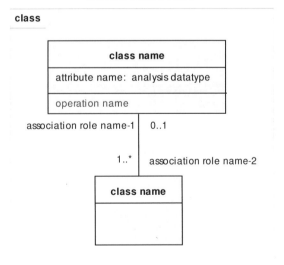

**(just the line between the two Class icons and the association role names and multiplicities)**

| Informal definition | A general relationship between two diagram nodes (e.g., Class icons when used in Class models). |
|---|---|

| Used in diagrams | Class; Deployment; Use Case |
|---|---|
| Suggestions for use | Use this to document and name the relationship between the two classes and to indicate the multiplicities of the relationship. Association is the most frequently used relationship between classes. Aggregation and composition are more specific relationships, although the author recommends that they not be used for business analysis purposes. |

## *Composition*

**class composition**

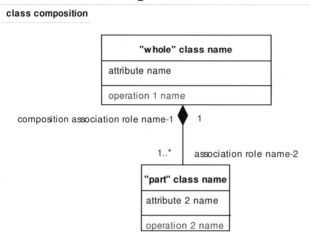

**(just the line between the two Class icons and its association role names and multiplicities)**

| Informal definition | A whole-part relationship where the "whole" class is made up of or contains the "part" class, and the "part" class can't exist without the "whole" class. The filled diamond is on the end of the whole/composite Class icon. |
|---|---|
| Used in diagrams | Class |
| Suggestions for use | Avoid the use of both aggregation and composition relationships for business analysis purposes: you don't need to use them, software developers devote inordinate amounts of time arguing over whether an association should be aggregation or composition, you'll need to explain the icons to business stakeholders, business stakeholders will argue over whether an association should be aggregation or composition, and they add no useful information to business stakeholders that can't be represented using appropriate association role names (e.g., contained in, part of, composed of). They are included so that if you ever come across them in diagrams created by software designers or developers, you'll recognize and understand them. |

| Diagram examples | none |
| --- | --- |

# *Generalization*

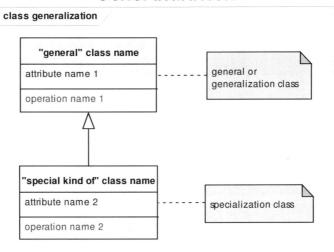

(just the line from the specialization Class icon to the general Class icon)

| Informal definition | A relationship in which the specialization class[17] contains all the properties (associations, attributes, and operations) of the generalization class[18], (the one pointed to by the triangle), plus more that are unique to it and do not apply to the generalization class. The generalization Class icon is pointed to by the triangle. For example, if you have two classes, Motor Vehicle and Motorcycle, since a motorcycle is "a special kind of" Motor Vehicle, a Generalization relationship between the two would have the triangle pointing to the Motor Vehicle. |
| --- | --- |
| Used in diagrams | Class, Use Case |
| Suggestions for use | Create a generalization class when there are some classes where most of their properties (attributes, operations, and associations) are identical, but some of the specialization classes have some different properties, or when there are just a few identical classes and visually displaying them all on a diagram helps your readers to verify you've identified them all. This option makes the different types visually explicit and clearly illustrates their differences. However, it does increase the size of the diagram. See the generalization item in the How-to-Model Tips section of this chapter for additional information. |

[17] known in data modeling as a subtype
[18] known in data modeling as a supertype

| Diagram examples | In Figure 2-1 UML diagram categories, the arrow from the Structure Diagram class to the UML Diagram class, and the arrow from the Behavior Diagram class to the UML Diagram class. Note that while they represent two separate generalization relationships and could be represented by two totally separate arrow lines, the lines were merged into a single arrowhead: that's a simplified and typical way of representing multiple generalization relationships to the same Class icon on a UML diagram. |
|---|---|

## Diagram Examples

Figure 8-1 vehicle registration, UML Class diagram, a business perspective UML Class diagram, indicates that a *vehicle owner* has a *name* with a datatype of *name-other*, a *street address* with a datatype of *text*, a *city name* with a datatype of *name-other*, a *state code* with the datatype of *code*, and a *zip code* with the datatype of *code*. Those are known as attributes (sometimes known as data elements in the non-UML world). The operations that can be performed on a *vehicle owner* are *add* (when a new *vehicle owner* is added to the system), and *change* (e.g., when a *vehicle owner's* address is modified in the system). A *vehicle owner owns* one or more *motor vehicles* (1..* is the multiplicity indicating a minimum of 1 and an upper bound of unlimited). Reading the association in the reverse direction indicates that a *motor vehicle* is *owned by* exactly one *vehicle owner*. Our fictitious Department of Motor Vehicles allows only a single owner. A *motor vehicle* is *registered by* one or many *motor vehicle registrations*. (The Somestate Dept of Motor Vehicles has a business rule that a new motor vehicle registration is issued each time a motor vehicle is purchased.) A *vehicle registration* is *paid for* by one or more *payments* (each renewal of a vehicle registration requires a payment). Each *payment pays* for exactly one *vehicle registration* (merely to keep the models simple, vehicle owners are not allowed to pay for two vehicle registrations with a single payment).

Note that the class names match the nouns in the Use Case Text Example of Chapter 5 Use Case Models. Also, the operation names match the verb portion of the Use Case names in Figure 5-1 vehicle registration, UML Use Case diagram: system use case.

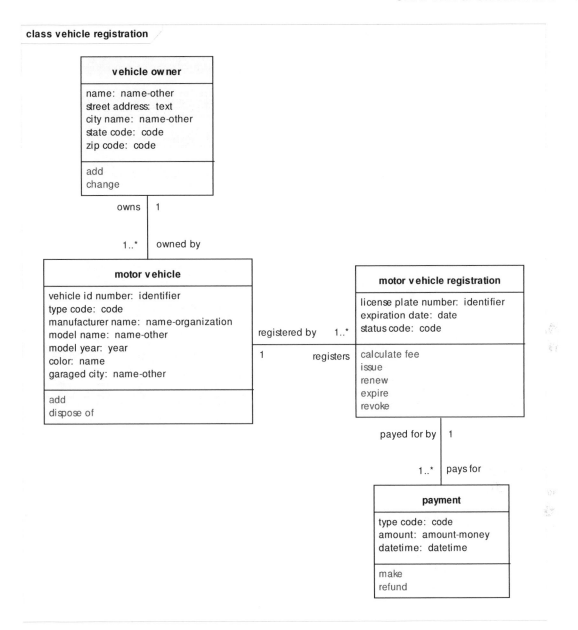

**Figure 8-1 vehicle registration, UML Class diagram**

Compare Figure 8-1 vehicle registration, UML Class diagram, a Class model with a business perspective, to the following Class model with a software implementation perspective. Figure 8-2 arguments, UML Class diagram fragment, software implementation perspective indicates that an *ArgList* (shorthand for argument list) has a *length* with a datatype of *int* (shorthand for integer) and operations of *Add* an *arg* (shorthand for argument, a software term for a parameter) returning an *ArgList*, *Get* returning an *arg*, *Set* an *arg*, *Remove* an *arg*. One special type of *ArgList* is *SingletonArgList*, which has an *element* with a datatype of *arg*. Another special type of *ArgList* is *TripletonArgList*, which has an *element0* with a datatype of *arg*, an *element1* with a datatype of *arg*, and an *element2* with a datatype of *arg*. Another special type of *ArgList* is *MultitonArgList*, which has a *contents* with a datatype of *List of arg*.

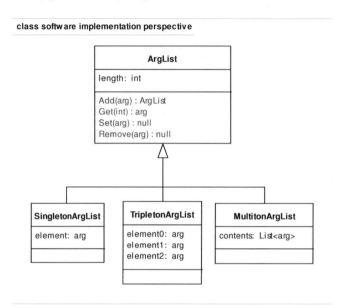

**Figure 8-2 arguments, UML Class diagram fragment, software implementation perspective**

## *Diagram Tips*

- Use consistent conventions for diagram layout:
  - The generalization Class icon above the specialization Class icons
  - The container Class icons above the contained Class icons
  - Person, organization, and place Class icons on the outside, events and business transaction Class icons near the center
  - The Class icons for the most important classes near the center of the diagram.
- Place the association role name from the source class and it's multiplicity to the target class on the same side (e.g., left, right, above, below) of the Association line. This makes it easier for people to read. For example, in Figure 8-1 vehicle registration, UML Class diagram *owns* at the *vehicle owner* class and *1..\** at the *motor vehicle* class are on the left side of the association line, making it easy for the reader to both think and

speak "a vehicle owner owns from one to many motor vehicles". Similarly, *owned by* at the *motor vehicle* class and 1 at the *vehicle owner* class are on the right side of the association line, making it easy for the reader to both think and speak "a motor vehicle is owned by one vehicle owner".

- To provide more information on the diagram, you can color-code the Class icons. Keep in mind that the colors are not useful when a diagram is printed in black and white and all colors print as shades of gray. An excellent color-coding methodology the author recommends is outlined in *Java Modeling in Color with UML* [Coad, 1999]. This book is primarily for experienced class modelers. The color scheme described in that book has nothing to do with the Java programming language.

- Use a consistent methodology for specifying attribute multiplicity. Three alternative conventions are described in the following sections.

  o Use the plural form of attribute name. The following business perspective UML Class diagram fragment uses the plural form of the attribute *color* to indicate a *motor vehicle* can have more than one *color*. This convention of indicating attribute multiplicities of greater than one has the advantages of being simple and requiring no explanation to typical business stakeholders, not adding clutter to the diagram, and requiring no special notation. The author recommends this convention when the target audience is subject matter experts. It may not be as well received by software developers, who are familiar with UML and prefer the typical UML multiplicity specification of [minimum value ... maximum value] and the added specificity that brings.

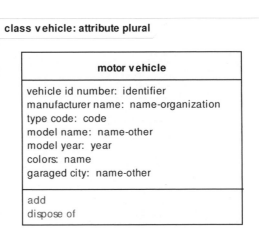

class vehicle: attribute plural

| motor vehicle |
| --- |
| vehicle id number:  identifier<br>manufacturer name:  name-organization<br>type code:  code<br>model name:  name-other<br>model year:  year<br>colors:  name<br>garaged city:  name-other |
| add<br>dispose of |

**Figure 8-3 motor vehicle, UML Class diagram fragment, attribute plural form**

o Use the standard UML format of [minimum value … maximum value] whenever the attribute multiplicity is not [1..1], the UML specified default value. The following business perspective UML Class diagram fragment uses the typical UML multiplicity specification of [lower bound .. upper bound] to indicate a *motor vehicle* may have from one to two colors. This convention has the advantages of using the same multiplicity notation for attributes as for associations, of being the notation that software developers familiar with UML would use, and of allowing more specificity (specifying the lower bound and specific upper bound (e.g., 2; note that using the plural form of an attribute name doesn't allow for specifying a maximum of two occurrences). The disadvantages are that it adds a notation that will likely require explanation to business stakeholders, it adds additional information to the diagram, and it takes up more space than using the plural form of an attribute name.

**class vehicle: attribute multiplicity**

| motor vehicle |
| --- |
| vehicle id number:  identifier<br>type code:  code<br>manufacturer name:  name-organization<br>model name:  name-other<br>model year:  year<br>color:  name [1..2]<br>garaged city:  name-other |
| add<br>dispose of |

Figure 8-4 motor vehicle, UML Class diagram fragment, attribute multiplicity specification

o Use standard UML format of [minimum value … maximum value] all the time. This is verbose and adds additional information to and takes up more space on the diagram than either of the previously noted conventions.

## Data Element List, Partial Example

The following table provides a partial example of a data element list used as a precursor to creating a Class model or data model, in this case the class model in Figure 8-1 vehicle registration, UML Class diagram.

**Table 8-2 Data Element List, Somestate Dept of Motor Vehicles, partial text example**

| Data Category | Data Element Name | Example Values | Analysis Datatype |
|---|---|---|---|
| motor vehicle | vehicle id number | 4Z1TM54879W303129 | identifier |
| | garaged in city | Mayberry | name-other |
| | manufacturer | Toyota | name-other |
| | model | Matrix | name-other |
| | year | 2008 | year |
| | color | White | name-other |
| vehicle registration | expiration date | 9/28/2013 | date |
| | license plate number | 537-HMT | identifier |
| | status | active, expired | code |
| owner | name | Jane Doe | name-person |
| | address | 123 Main St, Asheville, North Carolina, 27030-0913 | address |
| driver's license | driver's license number | S16987762 | identifier |
| | expiration date | 7/13/2014 | date |
| vehicle title | issue date | 11/19/2008 | date |
| payment | date | 9/15/2011 | date |
| | amount | $50.00 USD | money |
| | payment method | credit card | code |

## Class Model, Partial Text Example

The following table provides a partial example of a text version of the Class diagram in Figure 8-1 vehicle registration, UML Class diagram. For the sake of brevity, the associations and their association role names and multiplicity, and the attribute datatypes are not included, just the class and attribute definitions.

Table 8-3 Class Model Data Definitions, vehicle registration, partial text example

| Class name | Attribute name | Definition |
|---|---|---|
| vehicle owner | | The person or organization that owns a motor vehicle. |
| | name | The primary name of the vehicle owner (e.g., Somestate Highway Department, Joyce Smith). |
| | street address | The street or post office box portion of the postal address of the vehicle owner (e.g., 123 Main St, or P.O. Box 0329). Used to mail vehicle registration renewal notices. |
| | city name | The city portion of the postal address of the vehicle owner (e.g., Mayberry). Used to mail vehicle registration renewal notices. |
| | state code | The two character United State Postal Service state code for the state portion of the postal address of the vehicle owner (e.g., NC representing North Carolina). Used to mail vehicle registration renewal notices. |
| | zip code | The five or nine digit United States Postal Service zip code of the postal address of the vehicle owner (e.g., 27030-0913; or 01201). Used to mail vehicle registration renewal notices. |
| motor vehicle | | A motor vehicle registered by the Somestate Dept of Motor Vehicles System. |
| | vehicle id number | A manufacturer assigned identifier for a motor vehicle. Sometimes referred to as VIN (vehicle identification number). |
| | type code | A code categorizing the type of motor vehicle for use by Somestate Dept of Motor Vehicles System (e.g., A representing automobile, B representing bus, T representing truck) |
| | manufacturer name | The name of the manufacturer of the motor vehicle (e.g., Pontiac; Volkswagen) |
| | model name | The model name of the motor vehicle assigned by the manufacturer (e.g., Vibe, Prius) |
| | model year | The model year of the motor vehicle assigned by the manufacturer (e.g., 2009). |
| | color | The primary color of the motor vehicle (e.g., white). |
| | garaged city | The city in Somestate in which the motor vehicle is principally garaged (e.g., Mayberry). |

| Class<br>name | Attribute<br>name | Definition |
|---|---|---|
| motor<br>vehicle<br>registration | | A certification that the motor vehicle registration has been issued by the Somestate Dept of Motor Vehicles for a motor vehicle garaged in a city in the state. |
| | license plate<br>number | A unique identifier for a motor vehicle registration in the state. Displayed on the license plate. |
| | expiration<br>date | The date of expiration of the motor vehicle registration (e.g., 09/28/2011). |
| | status code | A code categorizing the status of the motor vehicle registration (e.g., A representing active, E representing expired, R representing revoked). |
| payment | | A payment made for a motor vehicle registration. |
| | type code | A code categorizing the payment method (e.g.,1 representing cash, 2 representing check, 3 representing credit card). |
| | amount | The monetary amount of the payment in US dollars (e.g., $35.00). |
| | datetime | The date and time a payment was received (e.g., August 17, 2011, 12:35 pm). |

## How-to-Model Tips

- Go for breadth first, then depth. Thus, identify the most important classes first, then their most important relationships, then their most important attributes and operations. Continue by adding the remainder of the classes, relationships, attributes, and operations, then add the text definitions to each class and attribute, and optionally assign an analysis datatype to each attribute.

- For business or domain models, look for items important to the business. These are typically the people, organizations, places, things, and events.

- Typically, the "event classes" are the central focus of domain Class models (e.g., appointment, conference, contract, meeting, performance, sale).

- Frequently, it's not just the person or organization that's important, rather their role or participation. For example, in `Figure 8-1 vehicle registration, UML Class diagram`, it's the vehicle owner that's important, rather than person or organization. For example, licensee and owner are the important concepts in a motor vehicle registry model while person and organization could be considered the classes that might be included in the model to play those roles.

- The author recommends against using aggregation or composition relationships for business analysis purposes. Should you decide to disregard that advice, avoid any protracted (i.e. longer than five minutes) debates over whether an association should be modeled as an aggregation or composition relationship. It's typically irrelevant for requirements purposes. When in doubt, don't make the association an aggregation or composition relationship.

- Although the author recommends against using them for business analysis purposes, should you elect to use aggregation or composition relationships, the multiplicity of aggregation and composition relationships is typically 1..1 or 0..1 at the "whole" end. For composition relationships it's 1..1 at the "whole" end.

- The author recommends using association role names, and using them all the time. For example, in `Figure 8-1 vehicle registration, UML Class diagram`, the association between vehicle owner and motor vehicle has a role name of "owns", indicating that the vehicle owner owns the motor vehicle, and another role name of "owned by", indicating that the motor vehicle is owned by the vehicle owner. UML also allows for an association name (optionally with an arrow pointing to one end of the association), however that is not as complete and informative as two association role names. Thus in `Figure 8-1 vehicle registration, UML Class diagram`, instead of the two association role names, the entire association between the *vehicle owner* and the *motor vehicle* could have been given an association name of "ownership", displayed in the middle of the association line. While sometimes association names are readily understandable, as in this case, not all associations have good association names, plus the use of the arrow to indicate direction adds another diagram icon that needs explaining to your readers. Thus the recommendation is to just use association role names. Keep in mind that your goal is to be consistent and include only enough information to make the diagram clear and unambiguous to your intended audience.

- To add additional information and be more precise, categorize each attribute using a standard set of analysis datatypes, such as those described in Appendix C Analysis Datatypes.

- Generalization guidance. There are several options for representing generalization. Three alternative methods are described in the following sections.

o Use just a type code when the different types have no different properties (attributes, operations, or associations), when there are many types, or to keep the diagram smaller and simpler than the other options allow. This is the simplest option because it doesn't increase the size of the diagram and provides no visual cues as to what the different types are. If you elect this option, make certain to document all of the different "types" either in the definition of the type code attribute or in the attribute's domain specification (the specification of the allowable values). For example, in `Figure 8-5 motor vehicle, UML Class diagram fragment, type code` all motor vehicles have those same attributes. A UML Note icon was used to list several of the "types".

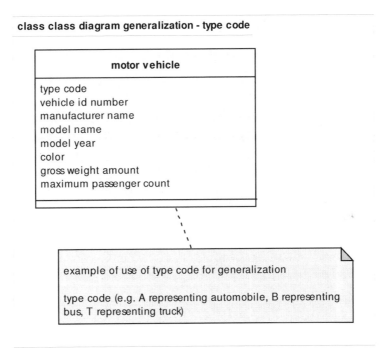

**class class diagram generalization - type code**

| motor vehicle |
| --- |
| type code |
| vehicle id number |
| manufacturer name |
| model name |
| model year |
| color |
| gross weight amount |
| maximum passenger count |

example of use of type code for generalization

type code (e.g. A representing automobile, B representing bus, T representing truck)

**Figure 8-5 motor vehicle, UML Class diagram fragment, type code**

o Create a generalization class when there are some classes with most properties (attributes, operations, or associations) identical, but some classes have some different properties, or when there are just a few classes with identical properties and visually displaying them all on a diagram helps your readers to verify you've identified them all. This option makes the different types visually explicit and clearly illustrates their differences; however, it does increase the size of the diagram. For example, in Figure 8-6 motor vehicle, UML Class diagram fragment, generalization relationship, the *truck* class has a *gross weight amount* attribute that other *motor vehicles* don't, and the *bus* class has a *maximum passenger count* attribute that other *motor vehicles* don't.

**class class diagram generalization - general class**

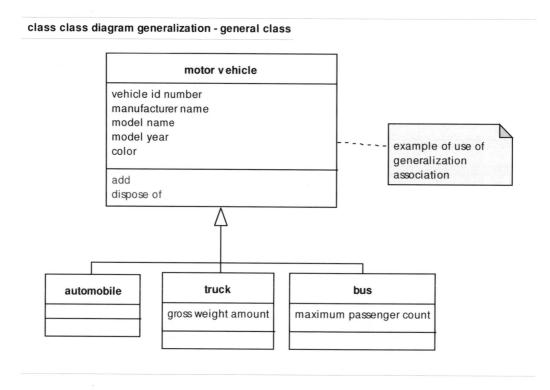

**Figure 8-6 motor vehicle, UML Class diagram fragment, generalization relationship**

o   Use a separate category or type class when there's more than just a single type code attribute, or when the system needs to explicitly manage different types (e.g., activate, inactivate a type). This option makes all the attributes, operations and associations that distinguish each type visually explicit, but does not make visually explicit the different types. For example, in Figure 8-7 motor vehicle, UML Class diagram fragment, category class the class *motor vehicle type* serves this purpose. A UML Note icon was used to list several of the "types".

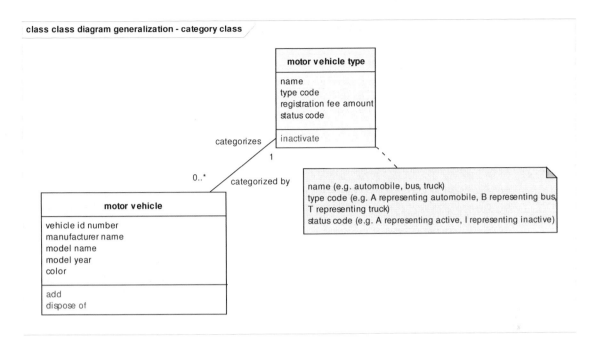

**Figure 8-7 motor vehicle, UML Class diagram fragment, category class**

## *Naming Guidelines*

- Name classes with a singular noun phrase, optionally prefixed with an adjective (e.g., motor vehicle, motor vehicle registration, vehicle owner).
- Name attributes with a noun phrase, typically in the singular (e.g., expiration date, model year, manufacturer name, status code). Use the plural form of the noun only if you adopt the convention of using the plural attribute name instead of the attribute multiplicity notation to indicate that the multiplicity of an attribute is more than one. Don't include the class name as part of the attribute name: the attribute is a property of the class and the fully qualified attribute name includes the class name. When written in text, an attribute name is typically prefixed by its class name and a period. Thus the attribute *expiration date* in the class *motor vehicle registration* is written "motor vehicle registration.expiration date".
- Name operations with an active voice, present tense verb phrase (e.g., calculate fee, dispose, issue, refund, renew, revoke). There is often no need for a direct object phrase, since the object of the verb is typically the class itself. For example, in the motor vehicle registration class, the operation name would be just "issue", rather than "issue motor vehicle registration". However, in the motor vehicle registration class, the operation name of "calculate fee" would be appropriate, rather than just "calculate".

"calculate expiration date" might also be an appropriate operation in the motor vehicle registration class.

- Name association role names on opposite ends of an association with complementary verb phrases. For example, "owns", an active voice verb in the present tense, at one end of the association; "owned by", a passive voice verb in the present tense at the other end of the association.

- General association role names such as "has", "related to", "associated with" indicate that there is no good name for the role, that you either haven't thought hard enough about the association, or that you don't understand enough about it to name it more specifically. These types of association role names should be used only as a last resort.

## Modeling Process Summary

The following is both a general process you may use as well as the process used to create the Class diagram in the next section.

The "Compare with related UML diagrams and adjust as appropriate" item in the following list is written under the assumption that you are creating a comprehensive and detailed model including all the UML diagram types and that you wish to have concepts covered in multiple diagram types whenever applicable. Thus suggestions such as "Confirm that all of the Lifeline icons in Sequence and Communication diagrams are represented as Actor icons in the Use Case diagrams. Add any missing Actor icons." may not apply in your situation.

1. List all the data elements.
   - Harvest these from the direct object phrase portion of use case names, from nouns in use case text, from Object Node icons in Activity diagrams, and from terms in a project glossary.
   - Include example value(s).
   - Categorize each data element into an analysis datatype, as defined in `Table C-1 Analysis Datatypes`.
   - Create an initial definition for each data element.
2. Place each data element under an appropriate data element category. See the Data Element List, Partial Example section in this chapter for an example.
3. Give each data element category a class name.
4. For each class name, identify the operations the actors or the system needs the class to perform.

- o Harvest these operation names from the verbs in use case names and use case text steps, the Action and Activity names in Activity diagrams, and the trigger event names in a State Machine model.

5. Draw the diagram.
   - o Add each Class icon and its attributes and operations. Be certain to add the definition for each class and attribute.
   - o Add any Generalization icons between each generalization Class icon and its specialization Class icons.
   - o Identify and add the Association icons between the Class icons.
   - o Add the association role name and multiplicity on each end of the association.

6. If the diagram will ever be viewed without its context information (current or future system, perspective, author, date created or last updated), add a UML Note icon similar to that in `Figure 3-1 UML Note`.

7. Compare with related UML diagrams and adjust as appropriate:
   - o Check if any direct object phrases from use case names are missing as Class icons. Check if any nouns from use case text should be added as attributes in classes.
   - o Check if any Object Nodes from Activity diagrams are missing as classes.
   - o Check if any Activities or Actions in Activity diagrams or use cases or use case steps should be represented by operations in the Class model.
   - o Confirm that all of the attributes in the Object diagram are included as attributes in the corresponding classes.
   - o Check if the status attributes whose values are represented by State icons in State Machine models or Timing diagrams are present in the appropriate class in the Class model.
   - o Check if any trigger events in the State Machine models are missing as operations in the appropriate class in the Class model.
   - o Check if any classes in a data model are missing from the Class model.

8. Review and verify the model with the appropriate stakeholders.

## Case Study Example Diagram

Here is an example of how you might describe the following business perspective UML Class diagram to your stakeholders, reading counterclockwise from the top left.

A *train pass reader* has a *serial number* that is used as an *identifier* and can *display a pass current value.*

A *train pass* has a *current monetary value,* and can be *purchased,* have *value added* to it, be *cashed in,* and can *have the fare value debited* from it.

A *train pass reader* can *read* from zero to many *train passes.* A *train pass* is *used in* from zero to many *train pass readers.*

A *train pass dispenser kiosk* has a *serial number* that is used as an *identifier,* and can *issue* a new *pass* and *add value to a pass.*

A *train pass* is *dispensed from* exactly one *train pass dispenser kiosk.* A *train pass dispenser kiosk dispenses* from zero to many *train passes.*

A *train* has a *number* that is used as an *identifier* and can *announce a station stop* (e.g., "The next stop is Braintree").

A *train run* has a *start datetime* and an *end datetime.*

A *train makes* from zero to many *train runs.* A *train run* is *made by* exactly one *train.*

A *stop* has an *arrival datetime* and a *departure datetime.*

A *train run includes* from one to eighteen *stops.* A *stop* is *included in* exactly one *train run.*

A *train station* has a *name* and an *operational status.*

A *train station* is the *site for* from zero to many *stops.* A *stop occurs at* exactly one *train station.*

A *train line* has a *color name* and can be *opened* or *closed.*

A *train line includes* between twelve and eighteen *train stations.* A *train station* is *part of* one to two *train lines.*

A *train line* is *served by* zero to many *trains.* A *train travels on* exactly one *train line.*

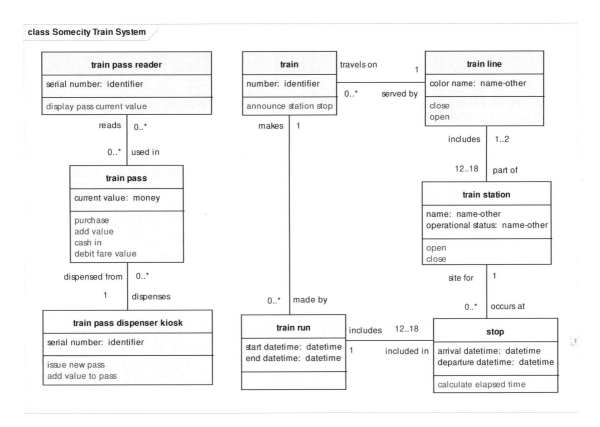

**Figure 8-8 case study, UML Class diagram, Somecity Train System**

## Relationship to Other UML Diagrams

- Classes may be found as the direct object phrase portion of a use case name, as the nouns in use case text, and as Object Nodes in an Activity diagram.
- Attributes may be found as nouns in use case text.
- "Status" attributes may be the subject of a State Machine model or Timing diagram.
- The values of a "status" attribute may be represented as states in a State Machine model or Timing diagram.
- An operation may be represented as an Action or Activity icon in an Activity diagram, as a trigger event in a State Machine model, or as a Use Case or series of steps of a Use Case.
- Some associations between classes may be indicated by the communication of a Message icon in a Sequence or Communication diagram.

Object diagrams show examples of the significant business entities (e.g., persons, places, events, concepts) that are relevant to the system (or business) under analysis, the relationships those entities have to each other, and example values of their data elements.

Object diagrams are similar to Class diagrams, except that they show specific instances of a class rather than just the class.

Object diagrams are not included in the BABOK Version 2.0 because they have not been used frequently by business analysts. However, the author has recommended that they be included in the next version.

## Purpose

Object diagrams should be used by business analysts to assist stakeholders in understanding Class models and data models. They accomplish that goal by including actual data values for the attributes, thus making them more concrete, and also by including multiple instances of a class to visually illustrate the multiplicities represented in a Class diagram by symbols (such as 0..*). They can also be used to illustrate how data values change over time, and how additional instances are added over time (e.g., the addition of another payment to an account). They may be used to illustrate a portion of the functional requirements.

Object diagrams show sample attribute values for a Class diagram, thus allowing readers to see a snapshot of data at a point in time.

Use Object diagrams to communicate with readers who prefer actual examples to abstract Class diagrams and terms, and when your readers are used to thinking in concrete values.

## Guidelines

Whenever you're creating a Class model or data model for a non-technical audience, create one or more corresponding Object diagrams to make the abstract concepts of a Class diagram clearer and more concrete.

Include actual names for classes when feasible. For example, if you have a class Person, name the object with a person's name (e.g., Jane Smith).

Use actual attribute values in the Object diagram. For example, if city is an attribute, include an actual city name (e.g., Cambridge).

## *Diagram Notation*

Become familiar with the following diagram elements for this diagram type. An example of most diagram elements is included in the first diagram of the Diagram Example section of this chapter. When that's not the case, the last row for that diagram element, labeled "Diagram examples", either includes one or more references to diagrams that contain that diagram element or indicates "none".

**Table 9-1 Object Diagram Notation**

The following icons fit into the **Diagram nodes** category:

## *Instance Specification (referred to in this book and elsewhere as an object or an instance of a class)*

object

| **object name : class name** |
|---|
| attribute name = attributevalue |

| Informal definition | An actual instance (or occurrence) of a class. For example, if the class were automobile, your car would be an instance of the automobile class. |
|---|---|
| Used in diagrams | Object |
| Suggestions for use | Use one of more Instance Specifications icons to illustrate instances of a class. This is the foundation of the Object diagram. |

The following icons fit into the **Diagram connectors** category:

## *Link* *(frequently referred to as association)*

**(just the line between the two instance specification/object icons)**

| Informal definition | A relationship between two objects, derived from the related association, aggregation, or composition relationship in the corresponding Class diagram. |
| --- | --- |
| Used in diagrams | Object<br>The similar appearing Association icon is used in UML Diagrams: Class; Component; Deployment; Use Case |
| Suggestions for use | Use to indicate an instance of one of the relationship types in Class diagrams: association, aggregation, composition. |

### *Diagram Example*

Figure 9-1 vehicle registration, UML Object diagram, a business perspective UML Object diagram, indicates that *Jane Doe*'s *mailing address* is in *Asheville, NC*, that Jane has a *2008 Pontiac Vibe*, and that this car has an *active motor vehicle registration* that will expire on *September 28, 2013*. A *payment* in the amount of *thirty-five dollars* for the registration was made on *September 27, 2009*, and a *payment* for a renewal of the registration was made on *September 15, 2011* in the amount of *fifty dollars*.

Note that the class and attribute names match the attribute names in the corresponding Figure 8-1 vehicle registration, UML Class diagram.

object vehicle registration

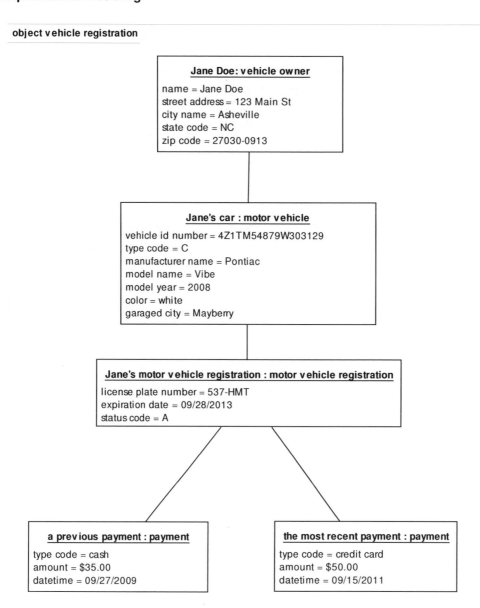

**Figure 9-1 vehicle registration, UML Object diagram**

## *Diagram Tips*

- As much as possible, the objects in an Object diagram should be placed where the corresponding Class icons are placed in the corresponding Class diagram.

- In a Class diagram, when there is a maximum multiplicity of greater than one (e.g., * representing many), use two or more (if necessary) of the corresponding objects in the Object diagram to illustrate that multiplicity.
- See the Diagram Tips section of Chapter 8 Class Models.

## *How-to-Model Tips*

- For each Object diagram, select a scenario or particular point you wish to illustrate (e.g., a single train run, a vehicle registration with the most recent payment and one older payment).
- First use the simplest and most typical examples possible to illustrate your point. Then create separate Object diagram(s) for exception cases, if appropriate.
- Determining the number of objects to create on an Object diagram is a delicate balance: don't include so few that the diagram doesn't illustrate multiplicities of greater than one, but don't include so many that the diagram is too cluttered to read easily.

## *Naming Guidelines*

- Object names consist of two optional portions, an instance name and a class name, separated by a colon (e.g., Jane Smith : Person). While both portions are optional, be consistent and include both to make it easier for the average person to understand. The colon must be included if only the class name is used, however, don't use just the class name. Instead, always use both so that you train your readers to expect to see the instance name every time.
- When stereotypical object names values are not appropriate, use "a" or "an" followed by the class name (e.g., a payment : payment; a hotel reservation : hotel reservation).
- Use actual sample attribute values whenever appropriate (e.g., payment amount = "$39.99", flight status = "cancelled").
- When actual sample values for an attribute are not appropriate, use stereotypical sample values (e.g., person name = "John Doe", birth date = "1/1/2001", credit card number = "1234 5678 9012 0000").

## *Modeling Process Summary*

The following is both a general process you may use as well as the process used to create the Object diagram in the next section.

The "Compare with related UML diagrams and adjust as appropriate" item in the following list is written under the assumption that you are creating a comprehensive and detailed model including all the UML diagram types and that you wish to have concepts covered in multiple diagram types whenever applicable. Thus suggestions such as "Confirm that all of the Lifeline icons in Sequence and Communication diagrams are represented as Actor icons in the Use Case diagrams. Add any missing Actor icons." may not apply in your situation.

1. Determine the purpose of the diagram.
2. Review the appropriate Class diagrams and determine which ones (or portions) warrant corresponding Object diagrams.
3. Add one Object (known in UML as an Instance Specification) icon and all the attributes for the corresponding class (except for generalization classes; for those, pick one of the specialization classes and add all of its attributes to the generalization class).
4. Add the associations (known as Links) for the corresponding associations in the Class diagram.
5. For those associations with upper bound multiplicity of greater than one, create a second Object icon.
6. Add the attribute values for each attribute in each Object. Use representative values, rather than exceptional values. However, you may leave attribute values empty if you're illustrating a situation where attributes must be empty. For example, leave the "actual departure date" unvalued if you're illustrating a hotel guest stay where the guest has not yet departed.
7. If the diagram will ever be viewed without its context information (current or future system, perspective, author, date created or last updated), add a UML Note icon similar to that in `Figure 3-1 UML Note`.
8. Compare the Object diagram with related UML diagrams and adjust as appropriate:
   o Confirm that all of the attributes from the corresponding class in a Class model are present in the corresponding Object icons.
   o Check that all of the attribute values of "status" attributes are present in the appropriate State Machine model.
9. Review and verify the model with the appropriate stakeholders.

## Case Study Example Diagram

Here is an example of how you might describe the following business perspective UML Object diagram to your stakeholders.

object train run

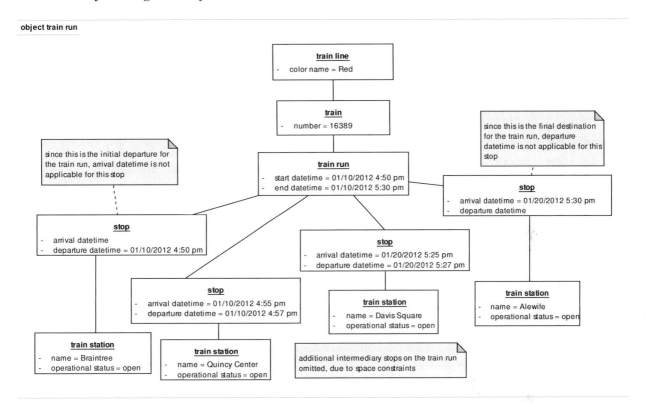

**Figure 9-2 case study, UML Object diagram, train run**

A *train line* has the *color name* of *Red*. That *train line* is associated with a *train* having a *train number16389*. That *train* is associated with a *train run* that had a *start datetime* of *January 10, 2012 at 4:50 pm*, and an *end datetime* of *January 10, 2012 at 5:30 pm*. That *train run* had an initial stop with a *departure datetime* of *January 10, 2012 at 4:50 pm* from the *Braintree train station* that had an *operational status* of *open*.

That *train run* also had a *stop* with an *arrival datetime* of *January 10, 2012 at 4:55 pm* and a *departure datetime* of *January 10, 2012 at 4:57 pm* at the *Quincy Center train station* that had an *operational status* of *open*.

There were additional intermediary stops.

That *train run* also had a *stop* with an *arrival datetime* of *January 10, 2012 at 5:25 pm* and a *departure datetime* of *January 10, 2012 at 5:27 pm* at the *Davis Square train station* that had an *operational status* of *open*.

That *train run* also had a final *stop* with an *arrival datetime* of *January 10, 2012 at 5:30 pm* at the *Alewife train station* that had an *operational status* of *open*.

## Relationship to Other UML Diagrams

- All the items in an Object diagram (except the attribute values) are found in the corresponding Class diagram.
- The attribute values are part of the domain (the specification of the allowable values) of the corresponding attribute in a data model.
- The values of a "status" attribute may be represented as states in a State Machine model or Timing diagram.

State Machine diagrams show all of the possible statuses of a business entity, plus all of the allowable changes between statuses with their associated constraints, typically referred to as business rules.

These diagrams are known by various names: statechart diagrams, state transition diagrams, Harel state charts, entity life cycle diagrams, life cycle diagrams.

State Machine diagrams are one of the techniques included in the BABOK Version 2.0.

## *Purpose*

State Machine diagrams may be used by business analysts in the requirements process to model the lifecycle history of an item (typically an instance of class in a Class model or an entity in a data model) by illustrating all of the possible changes between its allowable statuses (known in UML as states). They may be used to illustrate a portion of functional requirements.

State Machine models are sometimes used by software designers and developers to model the lifecycle of a software object (e.g., a window on a desktop application display).

## *Guidelines*

A State Machine model typically reflects the lifecycle of a single object of a class. A given instance may not visit each of the states in a State Machine model. However, the diagram contains all of the states and changes between them to represent the lifecycle of any instance, regardless of how unusual or rare that lifecycle may be.

If you find yourself wanting to include many state transitions that are not for the same object, you're probably modeling a business workflow or interactions. While State Machine diagrams may be used for that purpose, consider if an Activity diagram would be a better choice. If you need to illustrate the timing relationship between states of different objects, use a Timing diagram instead.

Because it typically includes decisions, branching, multiple different paths, and doubling back on previous actions, modeling of workflow is more appropriate with Activity diagrams than with State Machine diagrams.

While State Machine diagrams are a powerful technique for illustrating life cycles, life cycles can also be represented using State Machine tables. Some UML modeling tools will automatically generate one from the other. Compare the diagram representation in `Figure 10-1 vehicle registration`, `UML State Machine diagram` to the table representation of the same State Machine in `Table 10-2 State Machine table, vehicle registration`.

## *Diagram Notation*

Become familiar with the following diagram elements for this diagram type. An example of most diagram elements is included in the first diagram of the Diagram Example section of this chapter. When that's not the case, the last row for that diagram element, labeled "Diagram examples", either includes one or more references to diagrams that contain that diagram element or indicates "none".

**Table 10-1 State Machine Diagram Notation**

The following icons fit into the **Diagram nodes** category:

### *Final state*

stm

| Informal definition | An ending point for either a Region or an entire State Machine diagram. |
|---|---|
| Used in diagrams | State Machine |
| Suggestions for use | Whenever it doesn't make the diagram layout difficult to read, use only one Final state icon in a Region. It is easier for the readers of the diagram if there's a single end point, because they unconsciously recognize the commonalities of the multiple states that transition to a single Final state icon. Note that while Activity Final icon of an Activity diagram or Interaction Overview diagram and Final state icon of a State Machine diagram have the same visual appearance and serve analogous purposes, they represent different UML items. |

## *Initial Pseudostate*[19]

stm

| Informal definition | The starting point of a State Machine or Region. Referred to in this chapter as "start state". |
|---|---|
| Used in diagrams | State Machine |
| Suggestions for use | Use to indicate the beginning of a Region or a State Machine. There is no more than one for any Region of a State Machine diagram. Note that while the Initial Node icon of an Activity diagram or Interaction Overview diagram and the Initial Pseudostate icon of a State Machine diagram have the same visual appearance and serve analogous purposes, they represent different UML items. |

## *Region*

stm region

```
┌─────────────────────────────────┐
│          state name             │
│ [region 1 name]                 │
│                                 │
│ - - - - - - - - - - - - - - - - │
│ [region 2 name]                 │
│                                 │
└─────────────────────────────────┘
```

| Informal definition | A bounded portion of a State Machine diagram containing a set of states and state transitions, having exactly one Initial Pseudostate icon, having no more than one state active at a time, and separated from other Regions by dotted line(s). The above diagram includes the region names in brackets. A Region could be modeled as its own State Machine. |
|---|---|

---

[19] The reason it's named Initial Pseudostate rather than Initial State is not important for business analysis purposes and is beyond the scope of the book. The answer can be found in the UML metamodel in the UML superstructure specification.

| Used in diagrams | State Machine |
|---|---|
| Suggestions for use | Use Regions when you combine multiple State Machine diagrams for a single object into a single State Machine diagram in order to graphically illustrate the relationships among the states of those different State Machines. See `Figure 10-3 person, UML State Machine diagram, superstate with independent regions` for an example of a state containing two Regions. |
| Diagram examples | `Figure 10-3 person, UML State Machine diagram, superstate with independent regions` |

## *Simple state*

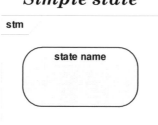

| Informal definition | A state that does not contain other states. |
|---|---|
| Used in diagrams | State Machine |
| Suggestions for use | This is the typical state category. Use whenever a state does not contain other states. |

The following icons fit into the **Diagram connectors** category:

## *Transition (referred to in this book as state transition)*

**(just the line between the source state icon and target state icon, plus its adornments: trigger event name, and guard condition)**

| Informal definition | The change from one state (referred to as the source state) to another (referred to as the target state). The transition includes a direction indicated by the arrowhead pointing to the target state icon, a trigger event name (e.g., renew), and optionally a guard condition, a condition that must be true in order for the change from the source state to the target state to occur (e.g., no unpaid parking fines). The trigger event initiating the state change is known in UML simply as "event". |
|---|---|
| Used in diagrams | State Machine |
| Suggestions for use | Use this to indicate an allowable change from the source state to the target state. |

The following diagram elements fit into the **Diagram other** category:

## *Duration Constraint, Duration Observation*

### {10..30 seconds} for a Duration Constraint; 2 hours for a Duration Observation

| Informal definition | A text specification of either a time duration for a Duration Observation (e.g., 2 hours), or a time duration range, for a Duration Constraint (e.g., {2..3 minutes}), optionally drawn with arrows extending to the lines indicating the start and end of the duration interval. |
|---|---|
| Used in diagrams | Sequence, State Machine, Timing |
| Suggestions for use | Use this to make a time duration or duration range explicit. Always include the unit of time (e.g., seconds, minutes). |
| Diagram examples | `Figure 11-1 pedestrian light, UML Timing diagram, state` `or condition timeline format,` `Figure 11-2 traffic light,` `UML Timing diagram, value lifeline format,` `Figure 11-3` `traffic light and pedestrian light, UML Timing diagram,` `state or condition timeline format,` and `Figure 11-4 case` `study, UML Timing diagram, train movement and door` `operation status, state or condition timeline format` for `Duration Observation.` |

## *Time Constraint, Time Observation*

### {1pm..2pm} for a Time Constraint; 2nd Friday of month at noon for a Time Observation

| Informal definition | A text specification for a point in time for a Time Observation (e.g., 2nd Friday of the month at noon), or a time interval for a Time Constraint (e.g., {1pm..2pm} optionally with arrows extending to each end of the time interval on the diagram). |
|---|---|

| Used in diagrams | Sequence, State Machine, Timing |
|---|---|
| Suggestions for use | Use to explicitly indicate a point in time specification or an interval of time, if appropriate. |
| Diagram examples | none |

## Diagram Examples

Figure 10-1 vehicle registration, UML State Machine diagram, a business perspective UML State Machine diagram, indicates that a vehicle registration when *issued,* as long as there is a *valid vehicle title,* is in the *active* state. An *active* vehicle registration can be *renewed* only if there are *no unpaid parking fines.* An *active* vehicle registration can be *suspended.* In order to *reinstate* a *suspended* vehicle registration there must be *no unpaid parking fines.* An *active* vehicle registration *expires* when its *expiration date is reached.* An *active* vehicle registration can be *revoke*d. There's no such thing as reactivating an expired vehicle registration or reinstating a revoked vehicle registration in the Somestate Dept of Motor Vehicles System.

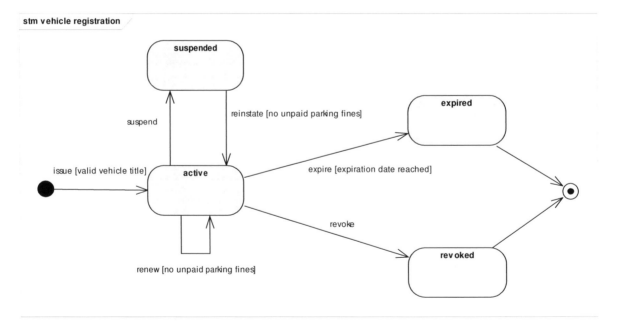

**Figure 10-1 vehicle registration, UML State Machine diagram**

Note that the trigger event names match the verb portion of the Use Case names in Figure 5-1 vehicle registration, UML Use Case diagram: system use case. Also, some of the guard conditions (e.g., no unpaid parking fines) correspond to the business rules identified in Use Case Text Example in Chapter 5 Use Case Models.

Figure 10-2 pedestrian light, UML State Machine diagram, superstate and substates, a business perspective UML State Machine diagram, indicates that when a pedestrian light is *installed* at an intersection, it is in the *inactive* state. When *activated*, it enters the *displaying 'don't walk'* state. While *active*, it can only be *inactivated* when it's in the *'don't walk'* substate. Clearly it's not safe to inactivate a pedestrian light while it's in the *displaying 'walk'* substate: pedestrians may be in the process of crossing the street! Similarly, a pedestrian light can only be *uninstalled* when it's in the *inactive* state. 'Active' is known as a superstate, since it contains other states; *displaying 'don't walk'* and *displaying 'walk'* are known as substates, since they are contained in another state. *Inactive, displaying 'don't walk'* and *displaying 'walk'* are known as simple states, since they don't contain other states.

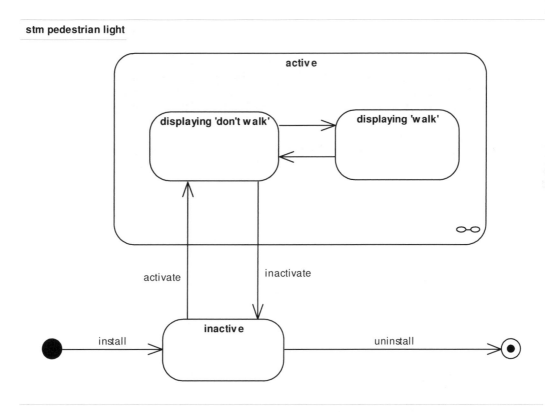

**Figure 10-2 pedestrian light, UML State Machine diagram, superstate and substates**

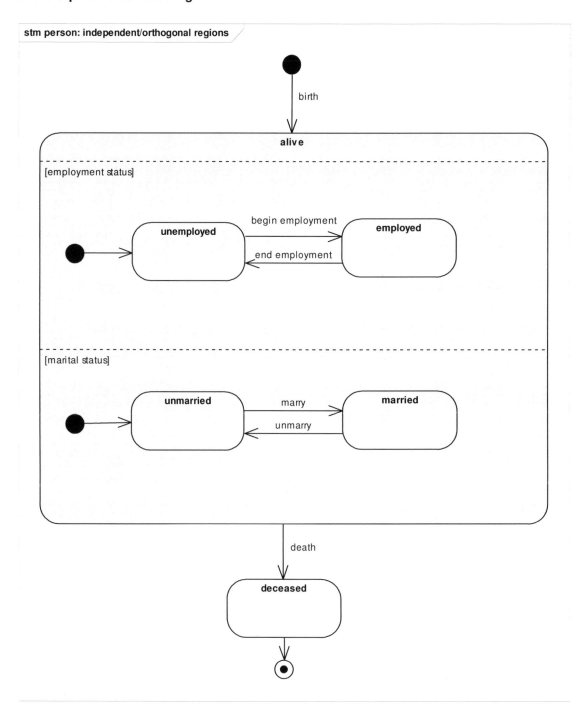

**Figure 10-3 person, UML State Machine diagram, superstate with independent regions**

Figure 10-3 person, UML State Machine diagram, superstate with independent regions, a business perspective UML State Machine diagram, indicates that a *birth* event places a person in the *alive* state. *Alive* (referred to in this book as a superstate, referred to in UML as a composite state) has two independent Regions (referred to in UML as orthogonal regions), *employment status* and *marital status*, meaning a person in the *alive* state also has both an *employment status* and a *marital status* at the same time. Since the Initial Pseudostate in *employment status* changes to *unemployed*, the *birth* event also changes a person to the *unemployed* state. Similarly, a person is *born* into the *unmarried* state. While *alive*, the person may change between *employed* and *unemployed*, and *married* and *unmarried* independently. At *death*, the person changes from the *alive* state to the *deceased* state. Note that this State Machine diagram could have been alternatively modeled as three separate State Machine diagrams, one for alive/deceased, one for employment status, and one for marital status. Since there are relationships between the three (e.g., a deceased person is no longer employed or married; when a person is born they are unemployed and unmarried), including all three on the same diagram utilizing Region icons graphically illustrates those relationships among the various states.

## Diagram Tips

- Use a consistent diagram layout convention, either left-to-right or top-to-bottom or topleftcorner-to-rightbottomcorner. For example, for left-to-right layout, place the "start state" icon on the left side of the diagram and a Final state icon on the right side.
- Avoid having state transition line cross, if possible. Including multiple Final state icons is one technique to accomplish this goal.
- Use a consistent methodology for state transition lines, e.g., state transition line angles may only be right angles; state transition lines may only use angles other than right angles, when necessary.
- Use a single "start state" icon in a diagram (or Region, if the diagram contains more than one Region).
- For each diagram (or Region if the diagram contains more than one Region) use a single Final state icon unless that would unnecessarily complicate the diagram. It makes it easy for readers if there is a single visual end point because they unconsciously recognize the commonalities of the multiple states that change to a single final state. If there are multiple states that change to the Final state icon and the state transition lines would make the diagram too cluttered for your readers to easily understand, utilize multiple Final state icons, but attempt to minimize the number of them.
- There are no state transition lines from a Final state icon.

## State Machine Table Example

Table 10-2 State Machine table, vehicle registration illustrates the use of a table to represent a State Machine. It represents the same information as in Figure 10-1 vehicle registration, UML State Machine diagram. A dash in the *final* state column indicates that the state transition from the corresponding state has no name.

**Table 10-2 State Machine table, vehicle registration**

| state\next state | initial | active | suspended | expired | revoked | final |
|---|---|---|---|---|---|---|
| initial | | issue [valid vehicle title] | | | | |
| active | | renew [no unpaid parking fines] | suspend | expire [expiration date reached] | revoke | |
| suspended | | reinstate [unpaid parking fines] | | | | |
| expired | | | | | | - |
| revoked | | | | | | - |
| final | | | | | | |

## How-to-Model Tips

- Look for statuses of items such as events, insurance policies, contracts, and relationships between different people and organizations. Then examine their status code values.
- Look for status code attributes in a Class model or a data model.
- Review use case text for the word "status". Search use case text for a list of common statuses, including those in the Naming Guidelines section of this chapter.
- Only create State Machine models for those classes/entities of relative importance and those with non-trivial State Machine models. For example,

don't bother creating a State Machine model for a class with just the state "active" or just the states "on" and "off".

- Use self-transitions for actions that occur, but the object remains in the same state ("revise" is a typical example of a self-transition). See the *renew* state transition in `Figure 10-1 vehicle registration, UML State Machine diagram` for an example.

- Use a superstate with substates to illustrate a hierarchical relationship between states. See the *active* state superstate with its substates of *displaying 'walk'* and *displaying 'don't walk'* in `Figure 10-2 pedestrian light, UML State Machine diagram, superstate and substates` for an example.

- When you have multiple State Machines for the same object, you can combine them into a single State Machine diagram with multiple Regions to graphically illustrate the various relationships among the various states. See `Figure 10-3 person, UML State Machine diagram, superstate with independent regions` for an example.

- Merged is typically not a state. Merge is frequently used to describe a process taken to resolve duplicate records of a single real world object. Should someone suggest including merged as a state, probe further to obtain a definition of that state and to understand the process that is used to resolve duplicate records. You will typically find that one of the records remains in its current state and will continue to be used, and the other record changes to an "obsolete", "inactive" or some other similar state, indicating that record should no longer be used in normal activities. Sometimes "merged" is one of the reasons, but not the only reason a record may be placed in an "inactive" state. Thus, "merged" is not the best name for the state, but "inactive" or "obsolete" may be better, more descriptive names for that state.

## *Naming Guidelines*

- In a State Machine diagram, it is preferable to name states using either gerunds (e.g., displaying, listening, moving, opening, running, starting, stopping, working) or past participles (e.g., cancelled, completed, dissolved, expired, revoked, stopped, suspended, terminated). Other typical state names include active, inactive, in force, in progress.

- Trigger event names should use verbs in the present tense. For example, complete, create, dissolve, expire, inactivate, renew, resume, revise, revoke, start, stop, suspend, or terminate.

- It is unnecessary to include the class or entity name in the trigger event name, since it's inherent. Thus, in a State Machine model for a life insurance policy, the trigger event name would be just "suspend" and not "suspend life insurance policy".
- Name guard conditions with a noun phrase (e.g., expiration date reached, no unpaid parking fines, reinstatement fee paid).

## Modeling Process Summary

The following is both a general process you may use as well as the process used to create the State Machine diagram in the next section.

The "Compare with related UML diagrams and adjust as appropriate" item in the following list is written under the assumption that you are creating a comprehensive and detailed model including all the UML diagram types and that you wish to have concepts covered in multiple diagram types whenever applicable. Thus suggestions such as "Confirm that all of the Lifeline icons in Sequence and Communication diagrams are represented as Actor icons in the Use Case diagrams. Add any missing Actor icons." may not apply in your situation.

1. Identify the class to which the State Machine applies.
2. Identify and list the different states that objects of that class can assume. These are frequently status values (e.g., active, inactive, suspended).
3. Identify, then group together any states that are part of a superstate.
4. Note any independent Regions, where an object can exist in one state from each of the Regions at the same time. See the *employment status* and *marital status* Regions of `Figure 10-3 person, UML State Machine diagram, superstate with independent regions` for an example.
5. Draw the diagram.
   - o Add the Initial Pseudostate icon.
   - o Add any Region icons.
   - o Add all State icons for superstates.
   - o Add all State icons for substates and simple states.
   - o Add the state transition lines between the source and target State icons, including any guard conditions for the state transitions.
   - o Add the Final state icon and any state transition lines to it.
6. Determine if the diagram could be included as a Region in a more comprehensive State Machine diagram. If so, decide if that is appropriate or if that would be too complex a diagram to review.
7. Compare with the related UML diagrams and adjust as needed:

- o Check if there are any use cases that represent state transitions, but are missing from the State Machine model.
- o Check if there are any Activity or Action icons from an Activity diagram that represent state transitions, but are missing from the State Machine model.
- o Check if there are any operations in the Class model that represent state transitions, but are missing from the State Machine model.
- o Check if there are any values in the "status" attributes from Object diagrams that are missing from the State Machine model.
8. Review and verify the model with the appropriate stakeholders.

## *Case Study Example Diagram*

Here is an example of how you might describe the following business perspective UML State Machine diagram to your stakeholders.

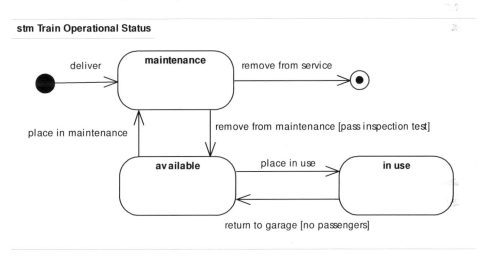

**Figure 10-4 case study, UML State Machine diagram, train operational status**

When a train is initially *delivered,* it enters *maintenance* status. When a train is *removed from maintenance* (as long as it has *passed its inspection test*) it enters *available* status. When a train in *available* status is *placed in maintenance,* it enters *maintenance* status. When a train in *available* status is *placed in use,* it enters *in use* status. When a train *in use* is *returned to the garage* (as long as it has *no passengers*), it returns to *available* status. A train in *maintenance* status may be *removed from service.*

## *Relationship to Other UML Diagrams*

- State Machine models can be used to verify Use Case models for completeness. Each state transition should be represented in one or more use cases or use case steps.
- A State Machine should be for one class in a Class model, typically one attribute (but more than one if Regions are included) in a Class model or data model.
- A trigger event may be represented by an operation of the applicable class, as an Activity or Action icon in an Activity diagram, or as a Use Case or series of use case steps.
- The states may be represented by attribute values in an Object diagram and the domain of an attribute in a data model.

Timing diagrams show the time duration of different statuses and, optionally, the timing relationships between the state transitions of different business entities.

Timing diagrams are one of the four diagram types in the UML Interaction diagram category.

Timing diagrams are not included in the BABOK Version 2.0 because they have not been used frequently by business analysts.

## *Purpose*

Timing diagrams may be used by business analysts to illustrate the business rules involving timing relationships, time durations, or time constraints between different states of an object or between the state transitions of different objects. They may be used to illustrate a portion of functional requirements.

## *Guidelines*

Timing Diagrams will be used infrequently for business analysis purposes. However they are helpful occasionally.

Use to visually illustrate the amount of time an object must remain in a given state.

Use to illustrate the time dependency between state transitions of different classes.

## *Diagram Notation*

Become familiar with the following diagram elements for this diagram type. An example of most diagram elements is included in the first diagram of the Diagram Example section of this chapter. When that's not the case, the last row for that diagram element, labeled "Diagram examples", either includes one or more references to diagrams that contain that diagram element or indicates "none".

**Table 11-1 Timing Diagram Notation**

The following icons fit into the **Diagram nodes** category:

## *General value lifeline*

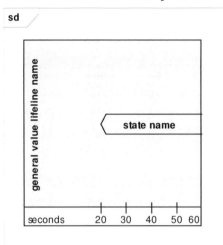

| Informal definition | A representation of the sequence of states of an object over time where the states are depicted by Xs sequenced horizontally. Not to be confused with Lifeline icons in Sequence and Communication diagrams. |
|---|---|
| Used in diagrams | Timing |
| Suggestions for use | Use to illustrate the length of time an object remains in a given state, or to illustrate the time dependency between states of different objects. General value lifelines and State or condition timelines are alternate representations of the same concept. You should use one format or the other. Don't confuse your readers by using two different diagram formats for the same concepts. |
| Diagram examples | Figure 11-2 traffic light, UML Timing diagram, value lifeline format, the entire section of crossing Xs labeled *displaying red, displaying green, displaying red*. |

## *State or condition timeline*

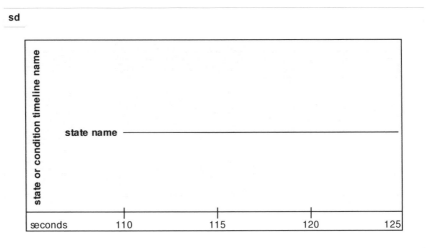

| Informal definition | A representation of the sequence of states of an object over time where the states are depicted by horizontal lines at different vertical levels. Not to be confused with Lifelines in Sequence and Communication diagrams. |
|---|---|
| Used in diagrams | Timing |
| Suggestions for use | Use to illustrate the length of time an object remains in a given state, or to illustrate the time dependency between states of different objects. Value lifelines and State or condition timelines are alternate representations of the same concepts. You should use one format or the other. Don't confuse your readers by using two different diagram formats for the same concept. |
| Diagram examples | Figure 11-1 pedestrian light, UML Timing diagram, state or condition timeline format, Figure 11-3 traffic light and pedestrian light, UML Timing diagram, state or condition timeline format, the two connected lines that cross the diagram. |

The following icons fit into the **Diagram** connectors category:

## *Message*

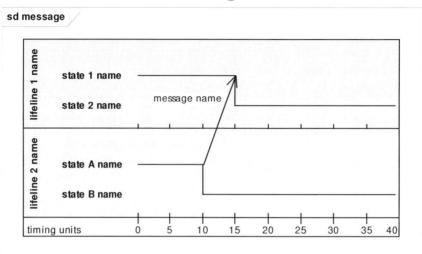

**(just the arrow between the two lifelines and its message name)**

| Informal definition | Represents a communication. |
|---|---|
| Used in diagrams | Communication, Sequence, Timing |
| Suggestions for use | Messages are seldom used in Timing diagrams created for business analysis purposes. They may be used to indicate a communication and its direction. There are three different types of messages, each with a slightly different icon. An asynchronous message (where the sender doesn't wait for a response) is indicated with an open arrow, as in the previous diagram. A call message (where the sender waits for a response) is indicated with a filled arrow, as in `Figure 12-3 case study, UML Sequence diagram, purchase train pass, main success scenario`, the *payment request* message. A reply message (one that is in response to a received call message) is indicated with a dashed line and an open arrow, as in `Figure 12-3 case study, UML Sequence diagram, purchase train pass, main success scenario`, the *payment response* message. |
| Diagram examples | `Figure 11-4 case study, UML Timing diagram, train movement and door` operation status, the *open door* and *start train* messages |

The following diagram elements fit into the **Diagram** other category:

# *Duration Constraint, Duration Observation*

**{10..30 seconds} for a Duration Constraint; 2 hours for a Duration Observation**

| Informal definition | A text specification of either a time duration for a Duration Observation (e.g., 2 hours), or a time duration range, for a Duration Constraint (e.g., {2..3 minutes}), optionally drawn with arrows extending to the lines indicating the start and end of the duration interval. |
|---|---|
| Used in diagrams | Sequence, State Machine, Timing |
| Suggestions for use | Use this to make a time duration or duration range explicit. Always include the unit of time (e.g., seconds, minutes). |
| Diagram examples | Figure 11-1 pedestrian light, UML Timing diagram, state or condition timeline format, Figure 11-2 traffic light, UML Timing diagram, value lifeline format, Figure 11-3 traffic light and pedestrian light, UML Timing diagram, state or condition timeline format, and Figure 11-4 case study, UML Timing diagram, train movement and door operation status, state or condition timeline format for Duration Observation. |

# *Time Constraint, Time Observation*

**{1pm..2pm} for a Time Constraint; 2nd Friday of month at noon for a Time Observation**

| Informal definition | A text specification for a point in time for a Time Observation (e.g., 2nd Friday of month at noon), or a time interval for a Time Constraint (e.g., {1pm..2pm}, optionally with arrows extending to each end of the time interval on the diagram). |
|---|---|
| Used in diagrams | Sequence, State Machine, Timing |
| Suggestions for use | Use this to explicitly indicate a point in time specification or an interval of time, if appropriate. |
| Diagram examples | none |

## *Diagram Examples*

Figure 11-1 pedestrian light, UML Timing diagram, state or condition timeline format, a business perspective UML Timing diagram in the state or condition timeline format, indicates that after the *pedestrian light* changes from *displaying 'don't walk'* to *displaying 'walk'*, it remains *displaying 'walk'* for 10 seconds before changing to *displaying 'don't walk'*. It remains *displaying 'don't walk'* for 75 seconds before changing to *displaying 'walk'*.

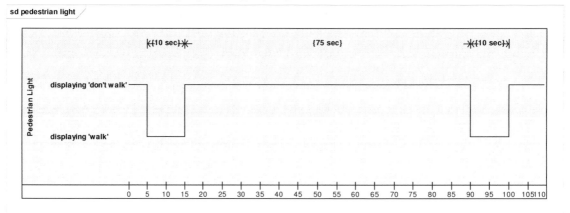

**Figure 11-1 pedestrian light, UML Timing diagram, state or condition timeline format**

Figure 11-2 traffic light, UML Timing diagram, value lifeline format, a business perspective UML Timing diagram in the value lifeline format, indicates that after a *traffic light* has been in the *displaying 'red'* state for 60 seconds, it changes to the *displaying 'green'* state. It remains in the *displaying 'green'* state for 25 seconds, before it changes to the *displaying 'red'* state.

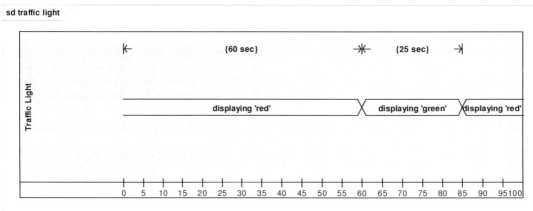

**Figure 11-2 traffic light, UML Timing diagram, value lifeline format**

Figure 11-3 traffic light and pedestrian light, UML Timing diagram, state or condition timeline format, a business perspective UML Timing diagram in the State or condition timeline format, illustrates the timing relationships between a *traffic light* and its *pedestrian light*. It indicates that *5 seconds* into the period when the *traffic light* is *displaying 'red'*, the *pedestrian light* begins *displaying 'walk'*. After *displaying 'walk'* for 10 seconds, the *pedestrian light* begins *displaying 'don't walk'*. Ten seconds after that (hopefully enough time for the pedestrians to finish crossing), the traffic light begins *displaying 'green'*. It continues *displaying 'green'* for 60 seconds. While the pedestrian light and traffic light Timing diagrams in themselves provided information, the combined Timing diagram of both the pedestrian light and traffic light enable visualization of the critical time relationships between the states of the two lights that help to ensure pedestrian safety!

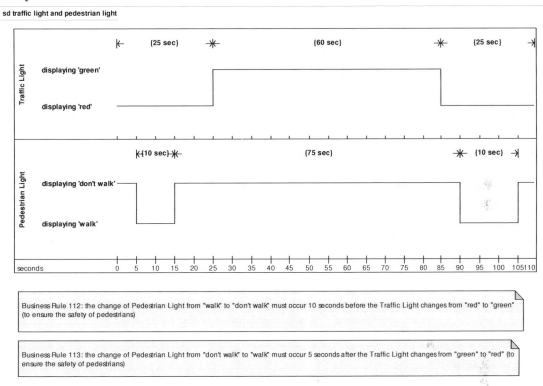

**Figure 11-3 traffic light and pedestrian light, UML Timing diagram, state or condition timeline format**

Note that the state names match the state names in `Figure 10-1 vehicle registration, UML State Machine diagram` and `Figure 10-2 pedestrian light, UML State Machine diagram, superstate and substates`.

## *Diagram Tips*

- There are two formats of Timing diagrams, State or condition timeline and General value lifeline[20]. The State or condition timeline format uses a

---

[20] The UML specification names the two formats "State or condition timeline" and "General value lifeline". The author is not convinced both formats shouldn't be labeled "timeline", or possibly "lifeline". This book uses the exact names from the UML specification.

different vertical height for each state and vertical lines to illustrate the state changes. The General value lifeline format displays all of the states with a set of parallel lines at the same vertical height and uses the crossing of the two lines to illustrate the state change.

- Unless there are specific reasons not to, select one of the two formats and only use that format. There's no reason to force your readers to learn two different diagram formats.
- In the State or condition timeline format of the diagram, dashed vertical lines can be optionally used to highlight the state changes.
- Label the timing durations and constraints with a time amount (e.g., 25 seconds) or a time interval (1-2 minutes). Always include the unit of measurement (e.g., seconds, milliseconds, minutes).

## How-to-Model Tips

- Identify the different state values and their timing durations.
- Identify any timing relationships between the state transitions of objects of different classes.

## Naming Guidelines

- Name states using the same naming guidelines as in Chapter 10 State Machine Models.
- Name the lifeline with a noun phrase (e.g., traffic light), which will typically be a class name in a Class model or a portion of or all of the corresponding status attribute name in the class (e.g., train movement for the train movement status attribute in the train class).

## Modeling Process Summary

The following is both a general process you may use as well as the process used to create the Timing diagram in the next section.

The "Compare with related UML diagrams and adjust as appropriate" item in the following list is written under the assumption that you are creating a comprehensive and detailed model including all the UML diagram types and that you wish to have concepts covered in multiple diagram types whenever applicable. Thus suggestions such as "Confirm that all of the Lifeline icons in Sequence and Communication diagrams are represented as Actor icons in the Use Case diagrams. Add any missing Actor icons." may not apply in your situation.

1. Decide whether to use the General value lifeline or State or condition timeline format.
2. Identify the lifeline(s) to be modeled.
3. Identify the timing range and timing unit (e.g., time range from 0 to 100 seconds).
4. Draw the diagram.
    o Add the Timeline icon with its timing range and timing unit.
    o Add the Lifeline icon(s).
    o Add the State icons and their state transitions to each Lifeline icon.
    o Add any Duration Constraints, Duration Observations, Time Constraints, or Time Observations.
    o Add any Message icons.
5. If the diagram will ever be viewed without its context information (current or future system, perspective, author, date created or last updated), add a UML Note icon similar to that in `Figure 3-1 UML Note`.
6. Compare the model with related UML diagrams and adjust as appropriate:
    o Ensure that state names match those from the applicable State Machines.
    o Ensure that the state names match the domain values of the applicable attributes of the data model.
7. Review and verify the model with the appropriate stakeholders.

## Case Study Example Diagram

Here is an example of how you might describe the following business perspective UML Timing diagram to your stakeholders.

When the *train movement* changes from *moving* to *stopped*, an *open door* message is sent. *Five seconds* later, the *door operation status* changes from *closed* to *open*. The *train door* remains *open* for *forty seconds*.

When the *door operation status* changes from *open* to *closed*, a *start train message* is sent. *Five seconds* later, the *train movement status* changes from *stopped* to *moving*. The *train movement status* had remained *stopped* for *fifty seconds*.

The Train Movement and Door Operation Interaction diagram illustrates the two business rules that the train must be stopped for five seconds before the door opens and that the doors must be closed for five seconds before the train begins moving.

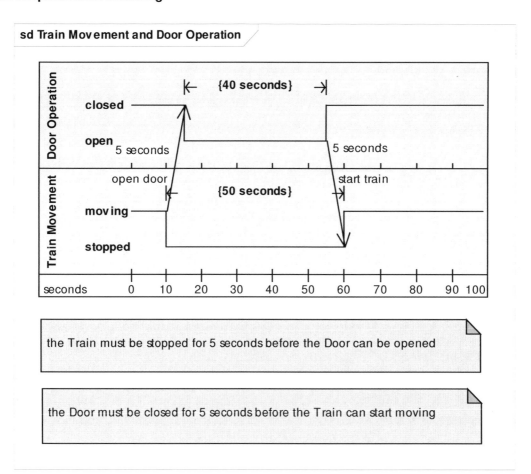

**sd Train Movement and Door Operation**

the Train must be stopped for 5 seconds before the Door can be opened

the Door must be closed for 5 seconds before the Train can start moving

**Figure 11-4 case study, UML Timing diagram, train movement and door operation status, state or condition timeline format**

## Relationship to Other UML Diagrams

- The states typically correspond to states in a State Machine model, and as the values of a "status" attribute in a Class model or data model.
- The lifelines typically correspond to classes in a Class Model or entities in a data model or lifelines in a Sequence or Communication diagram.

Sequence diagrams illustrate the time sequence of the information exchanges between various systems, and organizations and people roles.

They contain the interacting systems and the identification and ordering of the information exchanges between them.

Sequence diagrams are one of the four diagram types in the UML Interaction diagram category.

Sequence diagrams are one of the techniques included in the BABOK Version 2.0 to model "usage scenarios" (a series of steps, frequently those allowing an actor to accomplish a goal).

## Purpose

Sequence diagrams may be used by business analysts to illustrate the sequential flow of interactions or message exchanges for a single scenario. This would typically be a single use case scenario. They may be used to illustrate a portion of functional requirements.

A typical usage is to illustrate one use case scenario. Contrast this use of a Sequence diagram to illustrate one use case scenario with the use of an Activity diagram to illustrate all the possible scenarios of one use case.

Sequence diagrams are frequently used by software designers and developers to illustrate the messages passed between software objects during the execution of a scenario.

## Guidelines

The author recommends using Sequence diagrams only for system-to-system interactions, and only when you need to visually illustrate the sequence of those interactions (e.g., for a single use case scenario or part of one). The diagram layout of Sequence diagrams makes the time sequence extremely clear by the vertical positioning in the diagram. If you need to visually illustrate the sequence of person-to-system interactions, use an Activity diagram with Activity Partition icons and optionally, Object Node icons, instead; they're much better suited for visually illustrating alternatives and decisions. Use case text provides a text method of documenting person-to-system interactions when an Activity diagram would be too large or complicated.

Sequence diagrams can be used to indicate loops or conditional behavior, as illustrated in Figure 12-2 payment processing, UML Sequence diagram fragment, illustrating choice using an Interaction frame. However, the visual mechanism for showing loops and conditional behavior is suboptimal. When your Sequence diagram gets difficult to read due to loops or conditional behavior frames, use an Activity diagram to visually indicate conditional behavior, instead.

Sequence diagrams and Communication diagrams (when message numbers are included) contain the same information. Given one, you can create the other. Some modeling tools will automatically generate one from the other.

## Diagram Notation

Become familiar with the following diagram elements for this diagram type. An example of most diagram elements is included in the first diagram of the Diagram Example section of this chapter. When that's not the case, the last row for that diagram element, labeled "Diagram examples", either includes one or more references to diagrams that contain that diagram element or indicates "none".

**Table 12-1 Sequence Diagram Notation**

The following icons fit into the **Diagram nodes** category:

## *Interaction*

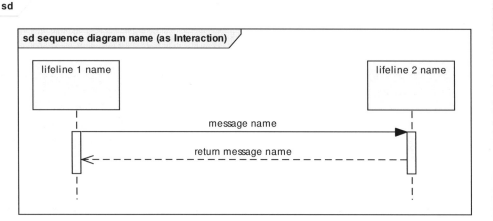

| Informal definition | An icon representing another diagram of the UML Interaction diagram category (Sequence, Communication, Timing, or Interaction Overview diagram) and including the icons of that referenced UML interaction category diagram. In the previous diagram fragment, the entire frame labeled "sd sequence diagram name (as Interaction)" is the Interaction (the frame contains a Sequence diagram). |
|---|---|
| Used in diagrams | Interaction Overview, Sequence |
| Suggestions for use | Although it is allowed, and can be used as described in the following paragraph, the author recommends not using an Interaction icon in a Sequence diagram to avoid complicating the Sequence diagram with another diagram icon type your readers will need to understand.<br><br>Use this to represent an Interaction specified outside of this diagram and include the diagram of that interaction. Sequence diagrams are the type of Interaction most frequently used; Communication diagrams, Timing diagrams, and Interaction Overview diagrams may also be used. Contrast the Interaction Use and Interaction icons and note that Interaction icons contain more information on the diagram. Utilize an Interaction icon if you have diagram space and want to include more details than an Interaction Use icon allows. |
| Diagram examples | `Figure 7-1 renew vehicle registration, UML Interaction Overview diagram`, the *check unpaid parking fines* Interaction and the *successful vehicle registration renewal* Interaction. |

## *Interaction Use*

**sd interaction use**

> **ref**
>
> interaction use name

| Informal definition | An icon representing another diagram of the UML Interaction diagram category (Sequence, Communication, Timing, or Interaction Overview diagram). The name of the Interaction Use refers to the other diagram being represented. In this diagram, the entire frame labeled "ref" is the Interaction Use. |
|---|---|
| Used in diagrams | Interaction Overview, Sequence |

| Suggestions for use | Although it is allowed, and can be used as described in the following paragraph, the author recommends not using an Interaction Use icon in a Sequence diagram to avoid complicating the Sequence diagram with another diagram icon type your readers will need to understand.<br><br>Utilize this to simplify a Sequence diagram by including less detail, or to conserve space in a Sequence diagram, or to factor out common behavior that can then be referenced (rather than duplicated) in other diagrams. Contrast the Interaction Use and Interaction icons and note that Interaction icons include more information on the diagram. |
|---|---|
| Diagram examples | Figure 7-1 renew vehicle registration, UML Interaction Overview diagram, the *obtain vehicle registration and vehicle owner information* and *process payment* Interaction Use, and Figure 7-2 case study, UML Interaction Overview diagram, purchase train pass details, the *obtain train pass desired amount information*, *pay with cash*, and *issue train pass* Interaction Use icons. |

## *Lifeline*

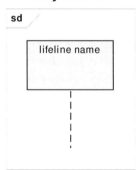

| Informal definition | Used to identify and name the message senders and recipients that participate in an information exchange. |
|---|---|
| Used in diagrams | Communication, Sequence |
| Suggestions for use | Use this to illustrate the senders and recipients of messages. Alternatively, the Actor icon from Use Case diagrams can be used for people lifelines to clearly distinguish them from system lifelines. |

The following icons fit into the **Diagram connectors** category:

## *Message*

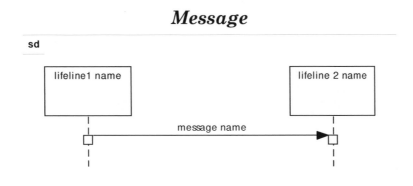

**(just the arrow between the two Lifeline icons and the message name)**

| Informal definition | Represents the information exchanged between two lifelines. |
|---|---|
| Used in diagrams | Communication, Sequence, Timing |
| Diagram examples | Figure 12-1 issue vehicle registration, UML Sequence diagram, main success scenario, *vehicle title query* and *unpaid parking fines query* representing call messages, *vehicle title response* and *unpaid parking fines response* representing reply messages. |
| Suggestions for use | Use this to indicate the data exchanged between the two lifelines and the direction of the data flow. There are three different types of messages, each with a slightly different icon. An asynchronous message (where the sender doesn't wait for a response) is indicated with an open arrow, as in Chapter 13 Communication Diagrams, the Message icon diagram fragment in the Diagram Notation section. A call message (where the sender waits for a response) is indicated with a filled arrow, as in Figure 12-3 case study, UML Sequence diagram, purchase train pass, main success scenario, the *payment request* message. A reply message (one that is in response to a received call message) is indicated with a dashed line and an open arrow, as in Figure 12-3 case study, UML Sequence diagram, purchase train pass, main success scenario, the *payment response* message. |

The following diagram elements fit into the **Diagram other** category:

## *Duration Constraint, Duration Observation*

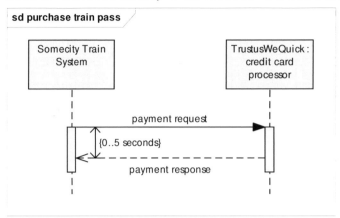

**(just the arrow with {0..5 seconds}, a Duration Constraint)**

| Informal definition | A text specification of either a time duration for a Duration Observation (e.g., 2 hours), or a time duration range, for a Duration Constraint (e.g., {2..3 minutes}, optionally with arrows extending to the lines indicating the start and end of the duration interval). |
|---|---|
| Used in diagrams | Sequence, State Machine, Timing |
| Suggestions for use | Use to make a time duration or duration range explicit. Always include the unit of time (e.g., seconds, minutes). |
| Diagram examples | Figure 11-1 pedestrian light, UML Timing diagram, state or condition timeline format, Figure 11-2 traffic light, UML Timing diagram, value lifeline format, Figure 11-3 traffic light and pedestrian light, UML Timing diagram, state or condition timeline format, and Figure 11-4 case study, UML Timing diagram, train movement and door operation status, state or condition timeline format for Duration Observation. |

## *Time Constraint, Time Observation*

**{1pm..2pm} for a Time Constraint; 2nd Friday of month at noon for a Time Observation**

| Informal definition | A text specification for a point in time for a Time Observation (e.g., 2nd Friday of the month at noon), or a time interval for a Time Constraint (e.g., {1pm..2pm}, optionally with arrows extending to each end of the time interval on the diagram). |
|---|---|
| Used in diagrams | Sequence, State Machine, Timing |
| Suggestions for use | Use to explicitly indicate a point in time specification or an interval of time, if appropriate. |

| Diagram examples | none |
|---|---|

## *Diagram Examples*

Figure 12-1 issue vehicle registration, UML Sequence diagram, main success scenario, a system perspective UML Sequence diagram, indicates that in the successful issuance of a vehicle registration, the *Somestate Dept of Motor Vehicles System* sends a *vehicle title query message* to the *Somestate Vehicle Title System*. The *Somestate Vehicle Title System* replies with a *vehicle title response message*. The *Somestate Dept of Motor Vehicles System* then sends an *unpaid parking fines query* message to the *Somestate Court System*. The *Somestate Court System* replies with an *unpaid parking fines response* message. The *Somestate Dept of Motor Vehicles System* then sends a *credit card payment request* message to the *Wecolekt Credit Card Processing System*, which returns a *credit card payment response*.

Note that the Lifeline icon names match the corresponding Actor names in Figure 5-1 vehicle registration, UML Use Case diagram: system use case and Activity Partition names in Figure 6-2 renew vehicle registration, UML Activity diagram, main success scenario.

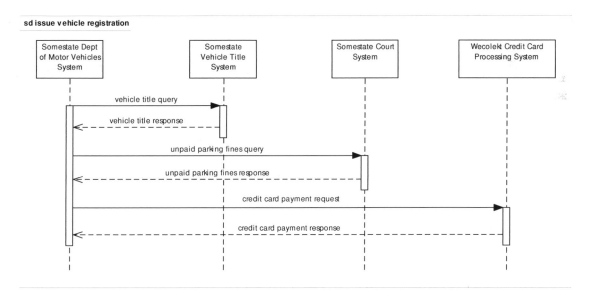

**Figure 12-1 issue vehicle registration, UML Sequence diagram, main success scenario**

Figure 12-2 payment processing, UML Sequence diagram fragment, a fragment of a system perspective UML Sequence diagram, indicates that the

*Somestate Dept of Motor Vehicles System* sends an *unpaid parking fines query* to the *Somestate Court System*, which replies with an *unpaid parking fines response*. If the *payment method* indicates *credit card*, the *Somestate Dept of Motor Vehicles System* sends a *request for credit card payment* to the *Wecolekt Credit Card Processing System*, the *Wecolekt Credit Card Processing System* sends a *credit card payment confirmation* back to the *Somestate Dept of Motor Vehicles System*. If the *payment method* indicates *check*, the *Somestate Dept of Motor Vehicles System* sends a *request for check payment* to *Weclearquik*, a *check clearinghouse*. *Weclearquik* responds with a *check payment confirmation*.

Note that the Lifeline icon names match the corresponding Actor names in `Figure 5-1 vehicle registration, UML Use Case diagram: system use case` and Activity Partition names in `Figure 6-2 renew vehicle registration, UML Activity diagram, main success scenario`.

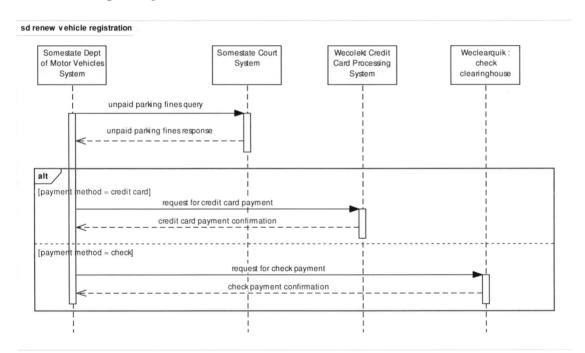

**Figure 12-2 payment processing, UML Sequence diagram fragment, illustrating choice**

## *Diagram Tips*

- Sequence the Lifelines in the order in which they appear in the scenario being modeled. If that results in too many partitions being crossed too many times by the message lines, simplify the diagram by reordering the partitions to minimize the number of lines crossing Lifeline icons.

- Sequence diagrams can get complicated and large. One way to simplify them is to substitute an Interaction Use icon for a portion of the Sequence diagram.

## How-to-Model Tips

- Determine the process to be modeled. Start at the beginning of the process to be modeled, and work your way through the sequence of interactions.
- People who are very concrete and find it difficult to think in abstract terms typically find it easier to verbally describe a process than to assist you in creating a diagram. When eliciting information from those people, you will likely need to capture their description of the process and use that information to create the Sequence diagram.
- Keep in mind that unlike in other UML diagrams, time progresses as you move down the diagram.

## Naming Guidelines

- The elements in a Sequence diagram are named in the same fashion as they are named in a Communication diagram.
- Name lifelines with the actual system name whenever they are known (e.g., Somestate Dept of Motor Vehicles System, Wecolekt Credit Card Processing System).
- If the actual system name is not yet known, use a generic system name generated by prefixing the generic system name with "a" or "an". For example, "a credit card processing system", if you know the external system is a credit card processing system, "a state court system" if you know the external system is a state court system.
- Lifeline names can use the same notation as object names in Object diagrams, objectname : classname. However, this naming convention is generally overkill (e.g., Wecolekt Credit Card Processing System : credit card processing system) and the two preceding naming guidelines are preferable.
- Message names can be named in two ways:
  - o a noun phrase naming the message or data content category (e.g., 820 Payment Order/Remittance Advice, payment request, payment confirmation)

o a verb phrase describing the intended action (e.g., check vehicle registration status)
- Be consistent and use just one of those methods. Your readers will appreciate the consistency.

## Modeling Process Summary

The following is both a general process you may use as well as the process used to create the Sequence diagram in the next section.

The "Compare with related UML diagrams and adjust as appropriate" item in the following list is written under the assumption that you are creating a comprehensive and detailed model including all the UML diagram types and that you wish to have concepts covered in multiple diagram types whenever applicable. Thus suggestions such as "Confirm that all of the Lifeline icons in Sequence and Communication diagrams are represented as Actor icons in the Use Case diagrams. Add any missing Actor icons." may not apply in your situation.

1. Identify the interaction to be modeled.
2. If there's an existing Communication diagram for the interaction, use that as the basis.
3. Identify all of the lifelines, the senders and receivers of the messages.
4. Identify the initial message and its sender and receiver.
5. Draw the diagram.
6. Add the Lifeline icon that sends the first message, then the Lifeline icon that receives that message, then the Message icon.
7. For the next message in the sequence, if not already present, add the Lifeline icon that sends the message; if not already present, add the Lifeline icon that receives the message; and finally, add the Message icon. Repeat this step until you've added all of the messages.
8. If the diagram will ever be viewed without its context information (current or future system, perspective, author, date created or last updated), add a UML Note icon similar to that in Figure 3-1 UML Note.
9. Compare with related UML diagrams and adjust as appropriate:
   o Check if there are either any flows across Activity Partition icons or Object Node icons in an Activity diagram that should be represented as Message icons between the corresponding Lifeline icons in the Sequence diagram.

        o   Check if there are any Lifeline icons or Message icons in Communications diagrams that should be added to the Sequence diagram.

10. Review and verify the model with the appropriate stakeholders.

## *Case Study Example Diagram*

Here is an example of how you might describe the following business perspective UML Sequence diagram to your stakeholders.

The *Somecity Train System* sends a *payment request* message to the *Trustuswequick credit card processor* system. The *Trustuswequick credit card processor* system replies with a *payment response* message within *zero to five seconds* of receipt of the *payment request* message.

Note that the Lifeline icon names match the corresponding Actor names in `Figure 5-1 vehicle registration, UML Use Case diagram: system use case` and Activity Partition names in `Figure 6-2 renew vehicle registration, UML Activity diagram, main success scenario.`

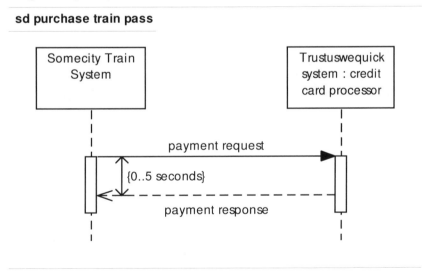

**sd purchase train pass**

**Figure 12-3 case study, UML Sequence diagram, purchase train pass, main success scenario**

## *Relationship to Other UML Diagrams*

- Lifelines may be represented as Actor icons in Use Case models.
- The sending of messages may be represented by use cases or steps in a use case, or as an Action or Activity icon in an Activity diagram.

- Activity diagrams utilizing Activity Partition icons and Object Node icons could be used to represent the information in a Sequence diagram. Keep your target audience in mind: software designers and developers are more likely to expect Sequence diagrams; business users will probably find Activity diagrams more familiar.

Communication diagrams show a summary of the flow of information between various systems, and organizations and people roles.

They contain the interacting systems and the identification and (optionally) ordering of the information exchanges between them.

Communication diagrams are one of the four diagram types in the UML Interaction diagram category.

Communication diagrams are not included in the BABOK Version 2.0 because they have not been used frequently by business analysts.

## *Purpose*

A Communication diagram created for business analysis purposes can be used to summarize the flow of information between the various systems.

Communication diagrams are used by software designers and developers to illustrate the messages passed between software objects during the execution of a scenario, when the associations are more important than the sequence of the messages.

## *Guidelines*

The only use the author suggests for business analysis purposes is a single Communication diagram for the entire system (or subsystem), including system Lifeline icons and actual message names, but no people Lifeline icons and no message numbers. Contrast this with the use of a Context diagram, which includes both system and people Lifelines icons, and data categories, rather than actual message names. `Figure 13-2 case study, UML Communication diagram, purchase train pass, main success scenario` illustrates the author's suggested usage.

Communication diagrams can be used to summarize the system-to-system information exchanges for an instance of behavior (e.g., for a single use case scenario or part of one), although a Sequence diagram is frequently a better choice. Use Sequence diagrams instead, when the focus of attention is on the time sequence of the messages exchanged between the lifelines. For example, `Figure 12-1 issue vehicle registration, UML Sequence diagram, main success scenario` clearly illustrates the time sequence of the messages exchanged since time goes forward as you move down the diagram. In contrast, `Figure 13-1 issue vehicle registration, UML Communication diagram` provides a summary of the messages exchanged between the lifelines, the time sequence being indicated by the message numbering.

Sequence diagrams and Communication diagrams (when message numbers are included) contain the same information. Given one, you can create the other. Some modeling tools will automatically generate one from the other.

## *Diagram Notation*

Become familiar with the following diagram elements for this diagram type. An example of most diagram elements is included in the first diagram of the Diagram Example section of this chapter. When that's not the case, the last row for that diagram element, labeled "Diagram examples", either includes one or more references to diagrams that contain that diagram element or indicates "none".

**Table 13-1 Communication Diagram Notation**

The following icons fit into the **Diagram nodes** category:

### *Lifeline*

| Informal definition | Used to identify and name the message senders and recipients that participate in an information exchange. |
|---|---|
| Used in diagrams | Communication, Sequence |
| Suggestions for use | Use this to illustrate the senders and recipients of messages. Alternatively, the Actor icon from Use Case diagrams can be used for people lifelines to clearly distinguish them from system lifelines. |

The following icons fit into the **Diagram connectors** category:

## *Message*

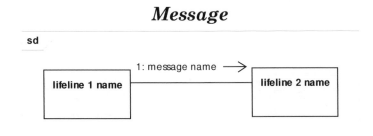

(just the line between the two Lifeline icons plus its adornments: the message sequence number, message name, and arrow indicating the direction of the message flow)

| Informal definition | Represents the information exchanged between two lifelines. |
|---|---|
| Used in diagrams | Communication, Sequence, Timing |
| Suggestions for use | Use this to indicate the data exchanged between the two lifelines and the direction of the data flow. Messages may be numbered to indicate their relative sequence (e.g., in a corresponding Sequence diagram). See Figure 13-1 issue vehicle registration, UML Communication diagram. There are three different types of messages, each with a slightly different icon. An asynchronous message (where the sender doesn't wait for a response) is indicated with an open arrow, as in the previous diagram fragment. A call message (where the sender waits for a response) is indicated with a filled arrow, as in Figure 12-3 case study, UML Sequence diagram, purchase train pass, main success scenario, the *payment request* message. A reply message (one that is in response to a received call message) is indicated with a dashed line and an open arrow, as in Figure 12-3 case study, UML Sequence diagram, purchase train pass, main success scenario, the *payment response* message. |

## *Diagram Example*

Figure 13-1 issue vehicle registration, UML Communication diagram, a system perspective UML Communication diagram, indicates that there are three groups of system-to-system information exchanges. The first two, between the *Somestate Dept of Motor Vehicles System* and the *Somestate Vehicle Title System*, involve the *vehicle title query* and its associated *vehicle title response*. The second two, between the *Somestate Dept of Motor Vehicles System* and the *Somestate Court System*, involve the *unpaid parking fines query* and its associated *unpaid parking fines response*. The third two, between the *Somestate Dept of Motor Vehicles System* and the *Wecolekt Credit Card Processing System*, involve a *credit card payment request* and its associated *credit card payment response*.

Note that the Lifeline icon names match the corresponding Actor names in `Figure 5-1 vehicle registration, UML Use Case diagram: system use case,` and Activity Partition names in `Figure 6-2 renew vehicle registration, UML Activity diagram, main success scenario.`

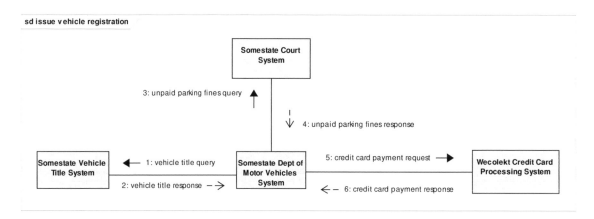

**Figure 13-1 issue vehicle registration, UML Communication diagram**

## *Diagram Tips*

- Place the system under analysis in the center.
- When feasible, layout the diagram in order from the left, based on the lowest message number. For example, place the system with the first message on the left in the 9 o'clock position, the system with next message in the 12 o'clock position, the system with the next message in the 3 o'clock position, etc.
- Messages may be numbered to indicate their relative time sequence (that would be obvious in a corresponding Sequence diagram). See `Figure 13-1 issue vehicle registration, UML Communication diagram` for an example. Compare the Communication diagram to the corresponding Sequence diagram in `Figure 12-1 issue vehicle registration, UML Sequence diagram` to understand the numbering sequence. While the UML specification allows for nested numbering of messages (e.g., 1, 1.1, 1.2, 2), the author has never found that necessary

when using Communication diagrams for business analysis purposes. When used to show a summary of the interactions, i.e. an "architectural view", and not the order of the messages, the author recommends not numbering the messages.

- When there are message pairs (e.g., a request message and its associated response message), place the request Message icon above its associated response Message icon if the association line is horizontal, or to the left of its associated response Message icon if the association line is vertical. People expect time sequences to be arranged left-to-right or top-to-bottom. `Figure 13-1 issue vehicle registration, UML Communication diagram` illustrates this positioning convention.

## How-to-Model Tips

- Determine the process to be modeled. Start at the beginning of the process to be modeled and work your way through the sequence of interactions.
- Some people find it easier to create a Sequence diagram first, then derive a Communication diagram from that.
- Some people find it easier to begin with a text description of an interaction. Then you can create the Communication diagram from the text description.

## Naming Guidelines

- The elements in a Communication diagram are named in the same fashion as they are named in a Sequence diagram.
- Name lifelines with the actual system name whenever they are known (e.g., Somestate Dept of Motor Vehicles System, Wecolekt Credit Card Processing System).
- If the actual system name is not yet known, use a generic system name generated by prefixing the generic system name with "a" or "an". For example, "a credit card processing system", if you know you the external system is a credit card processing system, or "a state court system", if you know the external system is a state court system.
- Lifeline names can use the same notation as object names in Object diagrams, objectname: classname. However, this naming convention is generally overkill (e.g., Wecolekt Credit Card Processing System : credit card processing system) and the two preceding naming guidelines are preferable.

- Message names can be named in two ways:
  - a noun phrase naming the message or data content category (e.g., 820 Payment Order/Remittance Advice, payment request, payment confirmation), or
  - a verb phrase describing the intended action (e.g., check vehicle registration status)

## *Modeling Process Summary*

The following is both a general process you may use as well as the process used to create the Communication diagram in the next section.

The "Compare with related UML diagrams and adjust as appropriate" item in the following list is written under the assumption that you are creating a comprehensive and detailed model including all the UML diagram types and that you wish to have concepts covered in multiple diagram types whenever applicable. Thus suggestions such as "Confirm that all of the Lifeline icons in Sequence and Communication diagrams are represented as Actor icons in the Use Case diagrams. Add any missing Actor icons." may not apply in your situation.

1. Identify the interaction or group of interactions to be modeled.
2. If there's an existing Sequence diagram for the interaction, use that as the basis.
3. Identify all of the lifelines.
4. Draw the diagram
   - Add all of the Lifeline icons.
   - Add the Message icons, labeling each Message icon with its message name, and add the direction of the message flow.
5. If the diagram will ever be viewed without its context information (current or future system, perspective, author, date created or last updated), add a UML Note icon similar to that in `Figure 3-1 UML Note`.
6. Compare with related UML diagrams and adjust as appropriate:
   - Check if there are either any flows across Activity Partition icons or Object Node icons in an Activity diagram that should be added as Message icons between the corresponding Lifeline icons in the Communications diagram.
   - Check if there are any Lifeline icons or Message icons in Sequence diagrams that should be added to the Communications diagram.
7. Review and verify the model with the appropriate stakeholders.

## Case Study Example Diagram

Here is an example of how you might describe the following business perspective UML Communication diagram to your stakeholders.

The diagram summarizes the information exchanges between the *Somecity Train System* and an external system, the *Trustuswequick credit card processor* system. There are two information exchanges between the *Somecity Train System* and the *Trustuswequick credit card processor* system. In one, the *Somecity Train System* sends a *payment request* to the *Trustuswequick credit card processor* system. In the other, the *Trustuswequick credit card processor* system sends a *payment response* to the *Somecity Train System*.

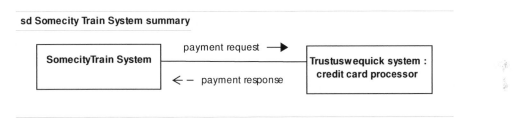

**Figure 13-2 case study, UML Communication diagram, purchase train pass, main success scenario**

## Relationship to Other UML Diagrams

- While Context diagrams and Communication diagrams may look similar, there are important differences to keep in mind. Context diagrams are at a higher level and present an overview of the information exchanges between the systems, identifying the data categories, but not identifying specific information exchanges. There's typically just one Context diagram for a system. Communications diagrams are at a lower level. They typically include the name of the messages exchanged between the systems and optionally the detailed order of the information exchanges, but not the data categories. There may be multiple Communication diagrams for a system to illustrate different scenarios.
- A Communication diagram can be thought of as a summary of a corresponding Sequence diagram. For example, `Figure 12-1 issue vehicle registration, UML Sequence diagram, main success scenario,` and `Figure 13-1 issue vehicle registration, UML Communication diagram` represent the same information.

- Communication diagrams can be used to summarize the interactions between all the actors in a Use Case model, although the author recommends not using them for that purpose because the Communication diagram would then effectively duplicate a Context diagram.
- Lifelines may be represented as Actor icons in Use Case models, or as Activity Partition icons in an Activity diagram.
- A message may be represented by an Object Node icon in an Activity diagram.

Composite Structure diagrams can be used either to illustrate the internal structure of a class or to show how different classes collaborate to accomplish a specific function.

They contain either the constituent parts of a software class or the different software classes that collaborate to accomplish a specific function.

Composite Structure diagrams are not included in the BABOK Version 2.0 because they have not been used frequently by business analysts and because they represent design rather than business requirements.

## *Purpose*

Composite Structure diagrams would not be created by business analysts as part of the requirements process. They are included so that if you ever come across them in diagrams created by software designers or developers, you'll recognize and understand them.

Composite Structure diagrams may be used by software designers and developers to either illustrate the constituent parts of a software class or the different software classes that collaborate to accomplish a specific function.

## *Guidelines*

Use this to illustrate either the internal structure of a class or how the classes communicate to accomplish the goal of the collaboration.

## *Diagram Notation*

Become familiar with the following diagram elements for this diagram type. An example of most diagram elements is included in the first diagram of the Diagram Example section of this chapter. When that's not the case, the last row for that diagram element, labeled "Diagram examples", either includes one or more references to diagrams that contain that diagram element or indicates "none".

**Table 14-1 Composite Structure Diagram Notation**

The following icons fit into the **Diagram nodes** category:

## *Class*

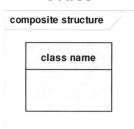

| Informal definition | A logical piece of software. Contrast this with the Class icon used in Class diagrams for business analysis purposes. |
|---|---|
| Used in diagrams | Class, Composite Structure |
| Suggestions for use | In Composite Structure diagrams, classes are frequently used to represent software artifacts (e.g., a query window, a message segment builder). |

## *Collaboration*

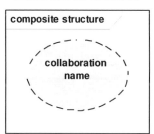

| Informal definition | A named collection of classes that together perform a task. |
|---|---|
| Used in diagrams | Composite Structure |
| Suggestions for use | Use this to illustrate how different classes work together to accomplish a specific function. |

The following icons fit into the **Diagram connectors** category:

## *Connector*

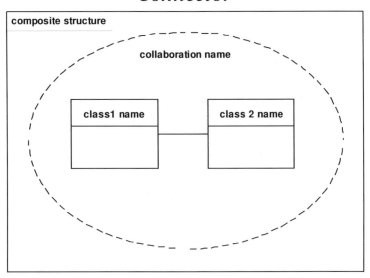

**(just the line between the two Class icons)**

| Informal definition | A connection between two classes indicating the two classes communicate to accomplish the goal of the collaboration. |
|---|---|
| Used in diagrams | Composite Structure |
| Suggestions for use | Use this to indicate a communication relationship between two classes. |

### *Diagram Example*

Figure 14-1 data interface processing collaboration, UML Composite Structure diagram, a system perspective UML Composite Structure diagram, illustrates the different classes that collaborate to receive and process a message and send an acknowledgement message. The *communication manager* class, acting in a *receiver* role receives a message, the *queue manager* class acting as an *inbound* queue accepts the message, the *data interface manager* class calls the *segment processor* class to process each of the message segments, then calls the *segment builder* class to assemble all the message segments for the acknowledgement message, the *queue manager* class acting as an *outbound* queue accepts the acknowledgement message, and the *communication manager* class, acting in a *sender* role sends the acknowledgement message. This illustrates that the same class can act in multiple roles (e.g., the *communication manager* class acts both as a message *receiver* and a message *sender*).

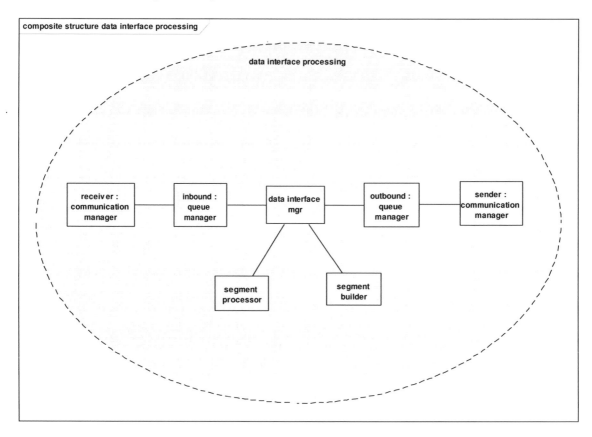

**Figure 14-1 data interface processing collaboration, UML Composite Structure diagram**

## How-to-Model Tips

Since these diagrams represent software classes or components, the software designers or software developers would need to provide all of the information to create one.

## Naming Guidelines

- Use a noun phrase to name the classes.
- Use a gerund or noun phrase to name the collaborations.

## *Modeling Process Summary*

The following is both a general process you may use as well as the process used to create the Composite Structure diagram in the next section.

1. Identify the collaboration to be modeled.
2. Identify the software classes and their connections that illustrate the collaboration.
3. Draw the diagram.
    - Add and name the Collaboration icon.
    - Add and name each of the software Class icons.
    - Add the Connector icons between the software Class icons.
4. If the diagram will ever be viewed without its context information (current or future system, perspective, author, date created or last updated), add a UML Note icon similar to that in Figure 3-1 UML Note.
5. Review and verify the model with the appropriate stakeholders.

## *Case Study Example Diagram*

Here is an example of how you might describe the following system perspective UML Composite Structure diagram to your stakeholders.

The data interface processing collaboration accepts an inbound message, processes it, and sends an acknowledgement message.

To accomplish that task, the *communication manager*, acting as a *receiver*, receives a message, the *queue manager*, acting as an *inbound* queue, accepts the message, the *data interface manager* interacts with the *segment processor* that processes each of the message segments, the *data interface manager* interacts with the *segment builder* which assembles all the message segments for the acknowledgement message, the *queue manager* acting as an *outbound* queue accepts the acknowledgement message, and the *communication manager*, acting in a *sender* role sends the acknowledgement message.

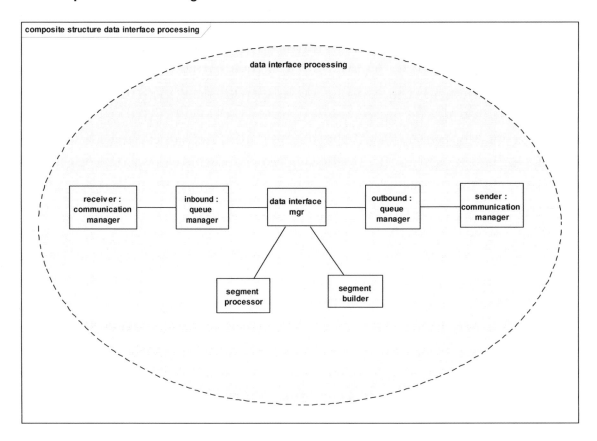

**Figure 14-2 case study, UML Composite Structure diagram, messaging component**

## Relationship to Other UML Diagrams

A Class icon can represent a software class in a Class model.

Component diagrams show the relationships between different software components.

Component diagrams are not included in the BABOK Version 2.0 because they have not been used frequently by business analysts and because they represent design rather than business requirements.

## *Purpose*

Component diagrams would not be created by business analysts as part of the requirements process. They are included so that if you ever come across them in diagrams created by software designers or developers, you'll recognize and understand them.

Component diagrams are used by software designers and developers to illustrate the structure of a single software component, or to illustrate relationships between software components or software systems with supplied and required interfaces.

Component diagrams created by software designers and developers may be read by business analysts to gain an understanding of the technical structure of the system in question, and could be helpful in understanding the scope of the solution software.

## *Guidelines*

A component is a collection of software that can be installed and replaced as a unit.

Avoid debates and unbeneficial discussions about the definition of a component.

The components may be coarse-grained (i.e. large scale) or fine-grained (small scale). For example, an accounts payable system would be a coarse-grained component (large in scope), while a time sheet would be a fine-grained component (smaller in scope).

## *Diagram Notation*

Become familiar with the following diagram elements for this diagram type. An example of most diagram elements is included in the first diagram of the Diagram Example section of this chapter. When that's not the case, the last row for that diagram element, labeled "Diagram examples", either includes one or more references to diagrams that contain that diagram element or indicates "none".

**Table 15-1 Component Diagram Notation**

The following icons fit into the **Diagram nodes** category:

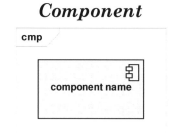

*Component*

| Informal definition | Software that can be implemented and replaced as a unit. Note that components can contain other components. |
|---|---|
| Used in diagrams | Component |
| Suggestions for use | Use this to indicate a software component. |

The following icons fit into the **Diagram connectors** category:

*Assembly*

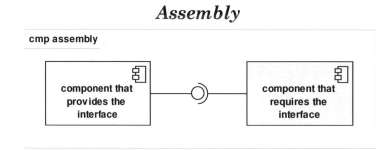

**(just the line between the two components with the "ball and socket" notation)**

| Informal definition | The association between a component that provides an interface and a component that requires the interface. |
|---|---|
| Used in diagrams | Component |

| Suggestions for use | Use to illustrate the association between a component that provides an interface and a component that requires the interface. The component that provides the interface is attached to the "ball" portion of the icon, the component that requires the interface is attached to the "socket" portion of the icon. |
|---|---|

## Diagram Example

Figure 15-1 messaging subsystem components, UML Component diagram, a system perspective UML Component diagram, indicates that there is a *queue manager* component that interacts with the *data interface manager* component through a *queue entry* interface. The *queue entry* interface is provided by the *queue manager* component and required by the *data interface manager* component. The *data interface manager* component interacts with the *segment builder* component through a *message segment* interface. The *data interface manager* component interacts with the *communications manager* component through a *message* interface.

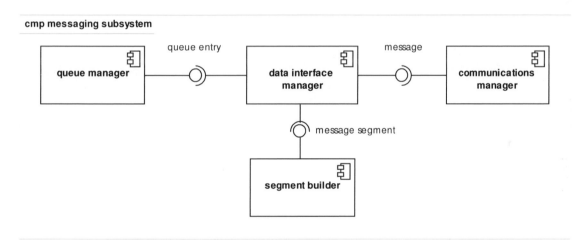

**Figure 15-1 messaging subsystem components, UML Component diagram**

## Diagram Tips

- A Component icon can be included in the top right corner of UML Component icons as was done in the diagrams in this chapter. Alternatively, the UML Component icons could include the UML keyword "component" in guillemets (e.g., «component»). Select the option that's most easily recognized and understood by your readers.

### How-to-Model Tips

Since these diagrams represent software components, the software designers or software developers would need to provide all of the information to create one.

### Naming Guidelines

- Components are named with noun phrases.
- Assemblies are named with noun phrases.

### Modeling Process Summary

The following is both a general process you may use as well as the process used to create the Component diagram in the next section.

1. Identify all of the components to be included.
2. Draw the diagram.
   o Add the Component icons.
   o Add the Assembly icons between the Component icons.
3. If the diagram will ever be viewed without its context information (current or future system, perspective, author, date created or last updated), add a UML Note icon similar to that in `Figure 3-1 UML Note`.
4. Review and verify the model with the appropriate stakeholders.

### Case Study Example Diagram

Here is an example of how you might describe the following system perspective UML Component diagram to your stakeholders.

The messaging subsystem contains a *queue manager* component that interacts with the *data interface manager* component through a *queue entry* interface. The *queue entry* interface is provided by the *queue manager* component and required by the *data interface manager* component. The *data interface manager* component interacts with the *segment builder* component through a *message segment* interface. The *data interface manager* component interacts with the *communications manager* component through a *message* interface.

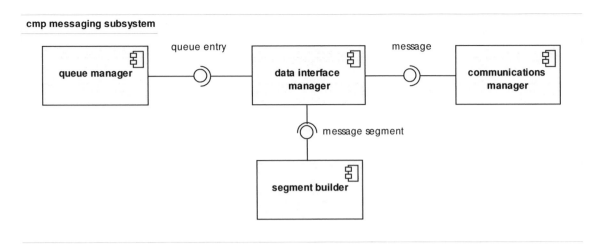

**Figure 15-2 case study, UML Component diagram, messaging subsystem components**

## *Relationship to Other UML Diagrams*

A component may be represented as a Component icon in a Composite Structure diagram.

Deployment diagrams illustrate how the devices and hardware nodes of a system are connected and, optionally, the software files residing on each of the hardware nodes.

Deployment diagrams are not included in the BABOK Version 2.0 because they have not been used frequently by business analysts and because they represent software implementation rather than business requirements.

## *Purpose*

Deployment diagrams would not be created by business analysts as part of the requirements process. They are included so that if you ever come across them in diagrams created by software designers or developers, you'll recognize and understand them.

Use this to illustrate the hardware nodes/processors/devices of a system, the communication links between them, and the placement of software files on those hardware nodes/processors/devices.

Use it to illustrate how a system will be physically deployed on the hardware.

## *Guidelines*

Identify the hardware nodes/processors/devices of a system, then the software files that reside on those nodes.

## *Diagram Notation*

Become familiar with the following diagram elements for this diagram type. An example of most diagram elements is included in the first diagram of the Diagram Example section of this chapter. When that's not the case, the last row for that diagram element, labeled "Diagram examples", either includes one or more references to diagrams that contain that diagram element or indicates "none".

Table 16-1 Deployment Diagram Notation

The following icons fit into the **Diagram nodes** category:

## *Artifact deployed on Node*

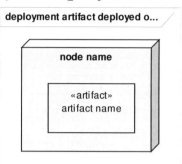

| Informal definition | Software files (e.g., executable files, scripts, HTML files, data files) physically present on a hardware node. In the above diagram fragment, the rectangle with the name "artifact name" and the stereotype of «artifact». |
|---|---|
| Used in diagrams | Deployment |
| Suggestions for use | Use this to indicate a software file present on a hardware node. |

## *Node*

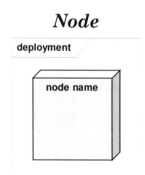

| Informal definition | Hardware on which software executes, such as an application server, a database server, a kiosk, etc. |
|---|---|
| Used in diagrams | Deployment |
| Suggestions for use | Use this to indicate servers, kiosks, etc. |

The following icons fit into the **Diagram connectors** category:

## *Association*

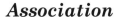

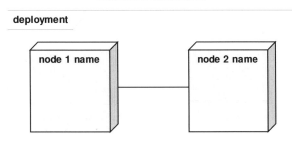

**(just the line between the two Node icons)**

| Informal definition | In Deployment diagrams, a representation of a communication link between the two hardware nodes. |
|---|---|
| Used in diagrams | Class; Deployment; Use Case |
| Suggestions for use | Use this to indicate a communication relationship between Node icons. |

### *Diagram Example*

Figure 16-1 Somestate Dept of Motor Vehicles System, UML Deployment diagram, a system perspective UML Deployment diagram, indicates that there is a *Maincity* node that communicates with both the *Mayfield* and *River City* nodes, as well as with the *Maincity kiosk* and the *Somestate Court System server*.

### *Diagram Tips*

- The associations between Node icons can be labeled with the type of network communication between them (e.g., http, SOAP over https).
- Instead of the stereotype name in guillemets (e.g. «server»), an icon representing the specific stereotype could be included on the Node icon. However this requires that your readers recognize the icons and what they represent, thus the author recommends using the stereotype name in guillemets.

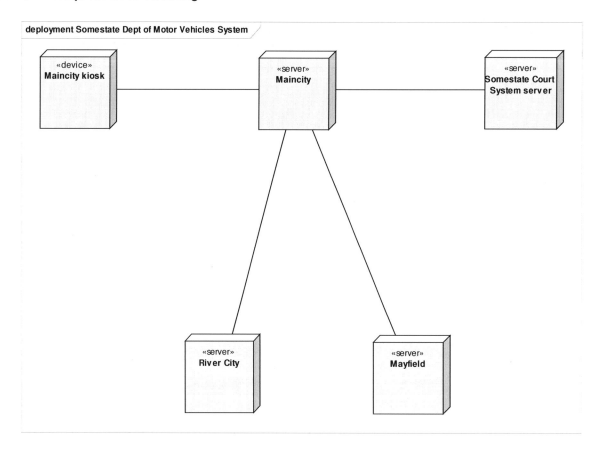

**Figure 16-1 Somestate Dept of Motor Vehicles System, UML Deployment diagram**

## How-to-Model Tips

- Since these diagrams represent software components and hardware nodes, the software designers or software developers would need to provide all of the information to create one.
- Use UML keywords to add additional information about a component or hardware node (e.g., «device»).
- Physical software artifacts (e.g., .exe files, .dll files, etc.) can be represented as artifacts on a hardware node.

## Naming Guidelines

- Hardware nodes and devices are named with a noun phrase. Hardware node names typically use a proper noun.
- Typically, the artifact name is the name of the file that the component represents.

## *Modeling Process Summary*

The following is both a general process you may use as well as the process used to create the Deployment diagram in the next section.

1. Identify all of the hardware nodes.
2. Draw the diagram.
   - Add and name all of the hardware Node icons. If applicable, add any applicable UML keywords such as «device».
   - Add all of the Association icons between the hardware Node icons.
3. If the diagram will ever be viewed without its context information (current or future system, perspective, author, date created or last updated), add a UML Note icon similar to that in `Figure 3-1 UML Note`.
4. Review and verify the model with the appropriate stakeholders.

## *Case Study Example Diagram*

Here is an example of how you might describe the following system perspective UML Deployment diagram to your stakeholders.

There is one *Somecity main system*. It is connected to one hundred instances of a *train pass reader device*. The *Somecity main system* is also connected to three hundred *train pass dispenser kiosks*. The *Somecity main system* is also connected to the *Trustuswequick system* using the *https* network protocol for secure http.

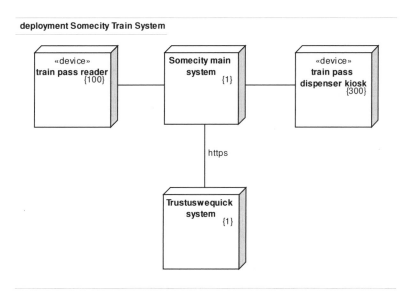

**Figure 16-2 case study, UML Deployment diagram, Somecity Train System**

## *Relationship to Other UML Diagrams*

A component may be represented as a Component icon in a Component or Composite Structure diagram.

Package diagrams show the hierarchical partitioning of a model into smaller parts, known in UML as Packages.

Package diagrams are not included in the BABOK Version 2.0, probably because they're not a generic technique, merely a mechanism to partition UML models.

## *Purpose*

Package diagrams may be used by business analysts to partition a model into functionally related groups, known in UML as Packages. For example, each subsystem could be placed in a separately named package containing all of the use cases, actors, classes, Use Case diagrams, Class diagrams, State Machine diagrams, etc. for that particular subsystem.

## *Guidelines*

For business analysis purposes, group functionally related items together into a single package. For example, place all of the use cases, Use Case diagrams, Class diagrams, State Machine diagrams, Sequence diagrams, etc. for vehicle registrations into one package, all those for driver's licenses into another package, all those for vehicle titles into another package.

Packages can be further divided into packages (i.e. you can nest packages). This is helpful for large models.

## *Diagram Notation*

Become familiar with the following diagram elements for this diagram type. An example of most diagram elements is included in the first diagram of the Diagram Example section of this chapter. When that's not the case, the last row for that diagram element, labeled "Diagram examples", either includes one or more references to diagrams that contain that diagram element or indicates "none".

**Table 17-1 Package Diagram Notation**

The following icons fit into the **Diagram nodes** category:

## *Package*

| Informal definition | A container that can be used to partition a model (e.g., into functionally related groups). |
|---|---|
| Used in diagrams | Package |
| Suggestions for use | Utilize packages to partition a large model into manageable parts. `Figure 17-1 Somestate Dept of Motor Vehicles System, UML Package diagram, not including package contents` partitioned the model into three packages: the vehicle registration package contains items related to vehicle registration, and driver's license contains items related to driver's licenses, and vehicle title contains items related to vehicle titles. While a package icon can be included in any other UML diagram, don't confuse your readers by doing that. However, including icons of the package contents in a Package diagram, as in `Figure 17-2 Somestate Dept of Motor Vehicles System, UML Package diagram, including package contents` is acceptable. |

## *Diagram Examples*

`Figure 17-1 Somestate Dept of Motor Vehicles System, UML Package diagram, not including package` contents, a UML Package diagram, indicates that there are three packages: one for *Vehicle Registratio*n, one for *Driver's License*, and one for *Vehicle Title*. There's no indication of what the packages contain.

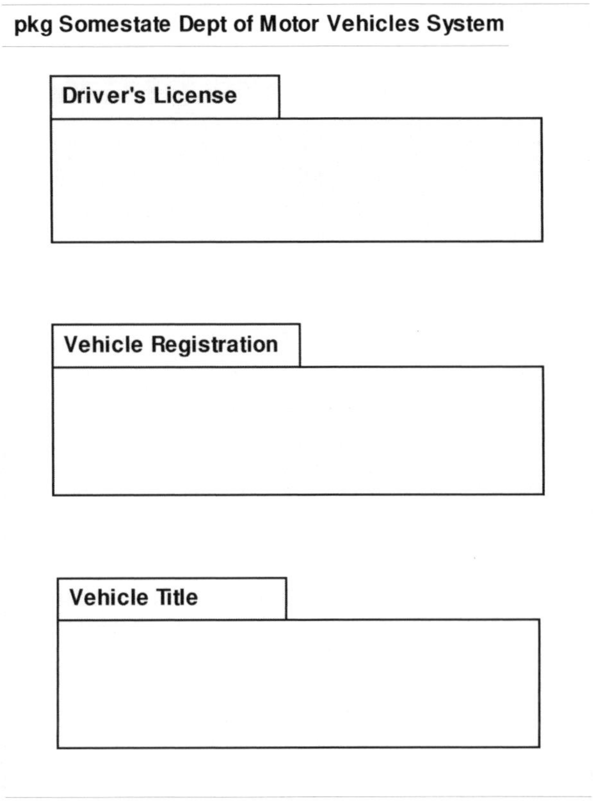

**pkg Somestate Dept of Motor Vehicles System**

**Driver's License**

**Vehicle Registration**

**Vehicle Title**

**Figure 17-1 Somestate Dept of Motor Vehicles System, UML Package diagram, not including package contents**

Figure 17-2 Somestate Dept of Motor Vehicles System, UML Package diagram, including package contents, a UML Package diagram, indicates that there are three packages: one for *Vehicle Registration*, one for *Driver's License*, and one for *Vehicle Title*. Each of the three packages displays the list of the Actor icons and Use Case icons contained in the package.

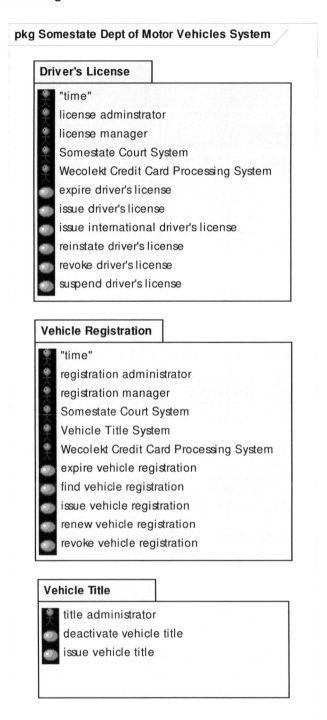

**Figure 17-2 Somestate Dept of Motor Vehicles System, UML Package diagram, including package contents**

## Diagram Tips

- Displaying the icons and names of the items included within a package within the Package icon is optional. Figure 17-1 Somestate Dept of Motor Vehicles System, UML Package diagram does not include the icons and names, whereas Figure 17-2 Somestate Dept of Motor Vehicles System, UML Package diagram, including package contents does include the icons and names. Don't include the icons and their names when it would create too much clutter on the diagram or make the diagram too unwieldy. Include the icons and their names when doing so doesn't make the diagram unwieldy or too cluttered.
- In typical UML modeling tools, you can navigate from the Package icon to its contents. For example, in Figure 17-2 Somestate Dept of Motor Vehicles System, UML Package diagram, including package contents, you can navigate from the package Vehicle Registration to the and use cases it contains.

## How-to-Model Tips

- Group related items together into a package. The categories you use to group will depend on your purpose and target audience. You might group items together in multiple ways for presentation to different audiences. When used for requirements purposes, there's no implication that the software itself will be developed using these groupings. The following are options for partitioning an entire model into packages:
    - o Create separate packages for functionally related items (e.g., vehicle registration, driver's license, vehicle title).
    - o Create a separate package for each subsystem (e.g., vehicle registration subsystem, driver's license subsystem, vehicle title subsystem).
    - o Create separate packages for system setup, ongoing operational activities, and reporting.
- Nest packages hierarchically to allow for partitioning and navigating a large model.

## Naming Guidelines

Name packages with a noun phrase (e.g., Vehicle Registration, Driver's License).

## *Modeling Process Summary*

The following is both a general process you may use as well as the process used to create the Package diagram in the next section.

1. Determine the criteria to use for breaking down a system into Packages (e.g., subsystem, business or workflow processes, related functions).
2. Identify all of the packages based on the criteria chosen.
3. Determine whether or not to include the list of package contents on the diagram.
4. Draw the diagram.
   o Add and name all of the Package icons.
5. If the diagram will ever be viewed without its context information (current or future system, perspective, author, date created or last updated), add a UML Note icon similar to that in Figure 3-1 UML Note.
6. Review and verify the model with the appropriate stakeholders.

## *Case Study Example Diagram*

Here is an example of how you might describe the following UML Package diagram to your stakeholders.

The *Somecity Train System* is divided into three logical packages: a *main processing subsystem*, a *web site subsystem*, and a *train pass subsystem*. Each of these logical packages contains a set of use cases, classes, Sequence diagrams, etc., although there's no indication of these contents in the diagram. Since this was intended to be an overview diagram, the contents of the packages are not listed in the Package icons on the diagram.

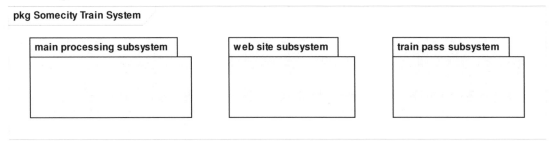

Figure 17-3 case study, UML Package diagram, Somecity Train System

## *Relationship to Other UML Diagrams*

All of the UML diagrams may be grouped into packages.

Context diagrams show the system or business under analysis, the external systems and person roles it interacts with, and the categories of data for each of the information exchanges.

Scope modeling is one of the techniques included in the BABOK Version 2.0. Context diagrams are one of the modeling notations mentioned, with Use Case diagrams and an overview-level business process model being the others.

Context diagrams are an extremely useful requirements tool for business analysis. They show what is in scope by its presence on the diagram, and indicate what is out of scope by what doesn't appear on the diagram. Context diagrams are not a part of UML. However, it makes sense for business analysts to utilize the same UML modeling tool for Context diagrams that they do for use case modeling and other UML models. Because UML Communications diagram notation can been utilized to create Context diagrams, this separate chapter is included.

## Purpose

Context diagrams are used by business analysts to document the system scope at a high level by illustrating the information exchanges between the system under analysis and the person roles and external systems with which it interacts.

## Guidelines

Since the typical goal is to model the scope of a system under analysis, include the other systems that interact with the system under analysis, but avoid including the systems that interact with the systems that interact with the system you're modeling. That can be an unending task. For example, in Figure 18-1 vehicle registration, Context diagram, the system under analysis is the *Somestate Dept of Motor Vehicles System*; while we include the *Wecolekt Credit Card Processing System* because it directly interacts with the *Somestate Dept of Motor Vehicles System*, we don't include any other systems that *Wecolekt Credit Card Processing System* interacts with.

Be aware that UML purists may balk at the use of UML Communication diagram notation for creating Context diagrams. Be certain to explain your adaption of the notation and label the diagrams Context diagrams, not Communication diagrams.

## Diagram Notation

Become familiar with the following diagram elements for this diagram type. An example of most diagram elements is included in the first diagram of the Diagram Example section of this chapter. When that's not the case, the last row for that diagram element, labeled "Diagram examples", either includes one or more references to diagrams that contain that diagram element or indicates "none".

**Table 18-1 Context Diagram Notation**

The following icons fit into the **Diagram nodes** category:

### *Lifeline*

sd

lifeline name

| Informal definition | The system under analysis, and the person roles and external systems with which it exchanges data. |
|---|---|
| Used in diagrams | Communication, Sequence |
| Suggestions for use | Use to represent the system under analysis, and the person roles and external systems that exchanges data with the system under analysis. |

The following icons fit into the **Diagram connectors** category:

### *Message*

**(just the line between the two Lifeline icons plus its adornments: data categories and direction)**

sd message

| Informal definition | The categories of information exchanged between the system under analysis and the person roles and external systems with which it interacts. |
|---|---|
| Used in diagrams | Communication, Sequence, Timing |
| Suggestions for use | Use this to indicate the data categories exchanged between the two lifelines and the direction of the data flow. While in a UML Sequence or Communication diagram there is a single message name, in a Context diagram you focus on categorizing the data and there will typically have multiple categories data, so use the data categories in place of a message name. Since the focus of a Context diagram is the categories of data, just use the UML asynchronous message type so that the direction of the data exchange is represented by the open arrows. While UML Communication diagrams may number the messages to correspond to the ordering of a corresponding Sequence diagram, numbering is not applicable in a Context diagram. |

## *Diagram Example*

Figure 18-1 vehicle registration, Context diagram, a system perspective Context diagram, indicates that, reading clockwise from the top left, the *registration administrator* provides *vehicle registration information, owner information,* and *payment information* to the *Somestate Dept of Motor Vehicles System.* The *SomestateDept of Motor Vehicles System* provides *vehicle registrations* and *payment receipts* to the *registration administrator.* The *Somestate Dept of Motor Vehicles System* provides *vehicle owner information* to the *Somestate Court System.* The *Somestate Court System* provides *unpaid parking fines* to the *Somestate Dept of Motor Vehicles System.* The *Somestate Dept of Motor Vehicles System* provides *vehicle identification information* to the *Somestate Vehicle Title System.* The *Somestate Vehicle Title System* provides *vehicle title information* to the *Somestate Dept of Motor Vehicles System.* The *Somestate Dept of Motor Vehicles System* provides *payment* information to the *Wecolekt Credit Card Processing System.* The *Wecolekt Credit Card Processing System* provides *payment confirmations* to the *Somestate Dept of Motor Vehicles System.* A *registration manager* provides *vehicle registration information* and *vehicle registration revocations* to the *Somestate Dept of Motor Vehicles System.* The *Somestate Dept of Motor Vehicles System* provides *vehicle revocation confirmations* to a *registration manager.*

Note that the external entity names match the corresponding Actor names in Figure 5-1 vehicle registration, UML Use Case diagram: system use case, the Activity Partition names in `Figure 6-2 renew vehicle registration, UML Activity diagram, main success scenario,` and the lifeline names in `Figure 12-1 issue vehicle registration, UML Sequence diagram, main success scenario` and `Figure 13-1 issue vehicle registration, UML Communication diagram.`

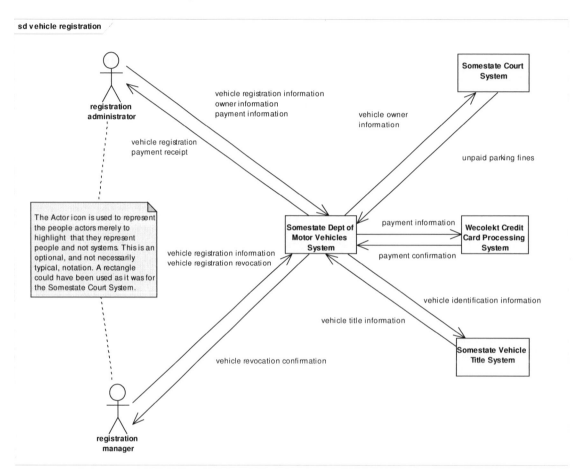

**Figure 18-1 vehicle registration, Context diagram**

## *Diagram Tips*

- Place the system under analysis in the middle. When that's not feasible use a UML keyword (e.g., «system» or «system under analysis»)) to distinguish the system under analysis from the external entities that exchange data with the system.
- If it makes sense and there's enough room, place people roles on one side of the system in question and external systems on the other side of the system in question.

- Use the Actor icon ("stick figure" used for actors in a Use Case diagram), rather than the standard Lifeline icon, for people roles so that your readers can easily distinguish them from the external systems. This is not a typical notation, so use it only if it makes sense to distinguish the people from the systems and document your use of this (e.g., with a UML Note icon). This convention is illustrated in `Figure 18-1 vehicle registration, Context diagram`.
- Use arrows to indicate the direction of the data flows.

## How-to-Model Tips

- Identify the different external systems. It's frequently helpful to think of the external systems that provide information to your system, and external systems from which your system needs to receive information.
- Identify the different categories of people who will be using the system. It's frequently helpful to think of those who will provide information to your system, and those who will receive information from your system.
- For each of the external systems, ask "is any data sent to that system?", then "is any data received from that system?"
- It's important to concentrate on the categories of data rather than how the data is packaged or presented. Thus, "company revenue" is better than "financial report" or "order header page".
- Use commonly accepted and well understood data categories, rather than individual data elements (e.g., payment information rather than payment amount, payment type, and payment datetime; vehicle owner information rather than vehicle owner name, vehicle owner street address, vehicle owner city name, vehicle owner state code, vehicle owner zip code). You may need to reference a glossary for those data categories, or create glossary entries for those data categories.

## Naming Guidelines

- For external systems, use the actual name of the system when it's well known among your readers. If the actual system name is not yet known, use a generic system name generated by prefixing the generic system name with "a" or "an". For example, "a credit card processing system", if you know you the external system is a credit card processing system, or "a state court system", if you know the external system is a state court system.

- For people roles, use the same names as in the Use Case diagram. See the Actor names portion of the Naming Guidelines section of Chapter 5 Use Case Models for details.
- For the data exchanged, use data categories rather than individual data element names.

## Modeling Process Summary

The following is both a general process you may use as well as the process used to create the Context diagram in the next section.

The "Compare with related UML diagrams and adjust as appropriate" item in the following list is written under the assumption that you are creating a comprehensive and detailed model including all the UML diagram types and that you wish to have concepts covered in multiple diagram types whenever applicable. Thus suggestions such as "Confirm that all of the Lifeline icons in Sequence and Communication diagrams are represented as Actor icons in the Use Case diagrams. Add any missing Actor icons." may not apply in your situation.

1. Identify all of the external systems and other actors that interact with the system.
2. Draw the diagram.
   - Add the system under analysis Lifeline icon in the middle.
   - Add all of the external systems and other actors as Lifeline icons around the system Lifeline icon.
   - For each of the external systems and actors, ask if they provide data to the system. If so, add a Message icon from the Lifeline icon representing the external system or actor to the Lifeline icon representing the system. Label the Message icon with the names of the data categories provided.
   - For each of the external systems and actors, ask if they receive data from the system. If so, add a Message icon from the Lifeline icon representing the system to the Lifeline icon representing the external system or actor. Label the Message icon with the names of the data categories provided.
3. If the diagram will ever be viewed without its context information (current or future system, perspective, author, date created or last updated), add a UML Note icon similar to that in `Figure 3-1 UML Note`.
4. Compare the model with the related UML diagrams and adjust as appropriate:

- o Check if there are any Actor icons in the Use Case diagrams that are missing from the Context diagram.
- o Check if there are any Activity Partition icons in the Activity diagrams that are missing from the Context diagram.
- o Check if there are any Lifeline icons in the Sequence diagrams or Communication diagrams that are missing from the Context diagram.
- o Check if there are any data categories from Object Nodes of Activity diagrams that missing from the Context diagram.
5. Review and verify the model with the appropriate stakeholders.

## Case Study Example Diagram

Here is an example of how you might describe the following business perspective Context diagram to your stakeholders.

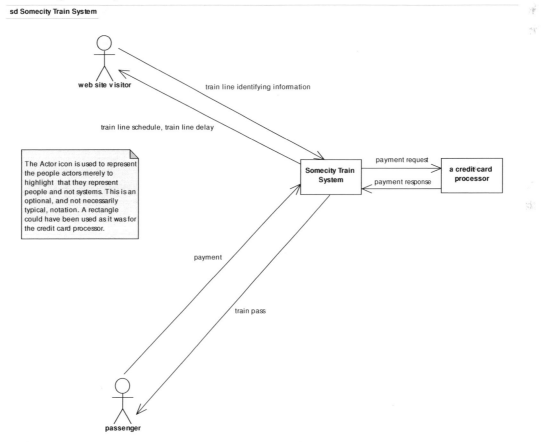

**Figure 18-2 case study, Context diagram, Somecity Train System**

A *web site visitor* provides *train line identifying information* to the *Somecity Train System*. The *Somecity Train System* provides *train line schedule, train line delay information* to the *web site visitor*.

A *passenger* provides *payment information* to the *Somecity Train System*. The *Somecity Train System* provides a *train pass* to a *passenger*.

The *Somecity Train System* provides *payment request information* to a *credit card processor*. A *credit card processor* provides *payment response information* to the *Somecity Train System*.

## Relationship to UML Diagrams

- While Context diagrams and Communication diagrams may look similar there are important differences to keep in mind. Context diagrams are at a higher level and present an overview of the information exchanges between the systems, identifying the data categories, but not identifying specific information exchanges; and there's typically just one Context diagram for a system. Communication diagrams are at a lower level, they typically include the name of the messages exchanged between the systems (but not the data categories), they may include the order of the information exchanges and they indicate response messages, and there may be multiple Communication diagrams for a system, illustrating different scenarios.
- An external entity represented by a Lifeline icon in a Context diagram may be represented by an Actor icon in a Use Case model, or an Activity Partition icon in an Activity diagram.
- A data category represented by a Message icon in a Context diagram may be represented by an Object Node icon in an Activity diagram.

Data models show the significant business entities (e.g., persons, places, events, and concepts) that are relevant to the system (or business) under analysis, the relationships those entities have to each other, and the information the business needs to capture about the business entities (referred to generally as data elements, and referred to in UML Class Models as attributes).

When used for business analysis, there are many similarities between Class models and data models. When used for business analysis, most of the guidelines and tips for data models also apply to Class models. Class models are treated separately in the Chapter 8 Class Models. Relevant material from that chapter is included in this chapter for the convenience of the reader.

Data models are a part of business analysis and are a useful requirements tool. Data model diagrams are not a part of UML. However, it makes sense for business analysts to utilize the same UML tool for data modeling that they do for use case modeling and other UML models. Because UML Class models have been adapted for use in data modeling, this separate chapter is included.

Data modeling is one of the techniques included in the BABOK Version 2.0. Class diagrams are listed as one of the modeling notations, with entity-relationship diagrams (ERD) being the other.

## Purpose

While object modelers and data modelers have different focuses and terminologies, fortunately for business analysis purposes, none of their disagreements affect your requirements modeling. Your primary goal is to produce a model of the items important to the business for the project, not a software design or database design. Thus, this book treats Class models and data models as similar, with the exception that Class models contain operations. Your object modelers can use your Class model as the basis for their software design. Your data modelers can use your Class model as the basis for their database design. You've assisted each of them in understanding the items important to the business for the project. Thus, when used for business analysis, all of the guidelines and tips for data models also apply to Class models.

Data models may be used by business analysts to create an analysis data model[21]. Thus they may be used to document the persistent data portions of functional requirements.

Data models are also used by data modelers and database designers to design a database, typically referred to as physical data models. Physical data models include the specification of primary keys, indices, partitions, etc. Since this category of data model represents system design, it is not covered in this book.

## *Guidelines*

Get assistance from an experienced data modeler if you are not familiar with data modeling.

Keep things as simple as possible to suit your purpose. For example, if the only need for a system is to display a telephone number to a person, represent the telephone number as single attribute. On the other hand, if your system is an international telecommunications system, you may need to represent telephone number as a class containing separate attributes for the country code (e.g., 1 or 8), area/city code (e.g., 800), and subscriber number (e.g., 555-1212) portions of a telephone number.

Simplify as appropriate. For example, if you need to include a full address (e.g., street address, city, state or province, zip or postal code, country) in multiple classes, you can just use an "address" attribute, but be certain to document somewhere how to break that down that compound attribute into its constituent parts.

Don't get caught up in advanced data model normalization techniques (e.g., 4th normal form, Boyce–Codd normal form) or defining primary keys. You are not designing a database; that is a task for a data modeler or database designer. You are providing a view of the data requirements that the system must support so that it can provide the functionality needed by the business. This view can be verified by the business stakeholders, and can be transformed into a database design by the database designers.

---

[21] The term "analysis data model" or "domain model" is used to refer to data models whose focus is just items important to the business, in contrast to a "physical data model" or a "database design data model".

While Scott Ambler has proposed a UML profile for data modeling that specifies a method for designating primary keys [Ambler, A UML Profile for Data Modeling], for business analysis purposes, avoid specifying primary keys, since that's a task best performed by database designers.

Instead of specifying primary keys, assign the analysis datatype value of identifier to an attribute of the business that by itself uniquely identifies an instance of the class. For example, in the Motor Vehicle class, assign vehicle id number the analysis datatype of identifier to indicate that knowing a motor vehicle's vehicle id number enables uniquely identifying a motor vehicle.

While designed for object oriented software, Class models are also well suited for modeling data requirements, irrespective of the target database management system.

While many traditional data modelers eschew the uses of the UML Class model notation in favor of traditional data model notations (e.g., Information Engineering, IDEF1X), others have adapted and embraced the use of UML Class models for data modeling. In particular, Scott Ambler was an early proponent [Ambler, Data Modeling 101], Michael Blaha recommends it [Blaha, 2010], and David Hay has written an analysis comparing traditional data modeling notations to UML Class models [Hay, 2011].

Just as in Use Case models, it's the text portion of a data model that often takes the longest amount of time. Constructing good definitions for classes and attributes takes considerable practice. Malcolm Chisholm has an entire book devoted to definitions [Chisholm, 2010].

Table 8-3 Class Model Data Definitions, vehicle registration, partial text example, lists the definitions of the classes and attributes of the associated Class diagram in Figure 8-1 vehicle registration, UML Class diagram.

### *Diagram Notation*

Become familiar with the following diagram elements for this diagram type. An example of most diagram elements is included in the first diagram of the Diagram Example section of this chapter. When that's not the case, the last row for that diagram element, labeled "Diagram examples", either includes one or more references to diagrams that contain that diagram element or indicates "none".

**Table 19-1 Data Model Diagram Notation**

The following icons fit into the **Diagram nodes** category:

## *Class*

class

| class name |
| --- |
| attribute name:  analysis datatype |

| | |
| --- | --- |
| Informal definition | An entity of importance to the business that also contains data elements. |
| Used in diagrams | Class, Composite Structure |
| Suggestions for use | Use a Class icon in requirements to indicate real world items (e.g., people, organizations, places, things, events, and business transactions). |

The following icons fit into the **Diagram connectors** category:

## *Association*

class

| class 1 name | | class 2 name |
| --- | --- | --- |
| attribute 1 name:  analysis datatype name | association role name 1      0..*  0..1         association role name 2 | attribute 2 name:  analysis datatype name |

**(just the line between the two Class icons and the association role names and multiplicities)**

| | |
| --- | --- |
| Informal definition | A general relationship between two diagram nodes (e.g., Class icons when used in Class models). |
| Used in diagrams | Class; Component; Deployment; Use Case |
| Suggestions for use | Use this to document and name the relationship between the two classes and to indicate the multiplicities of the relationship. |

## *Generalization*

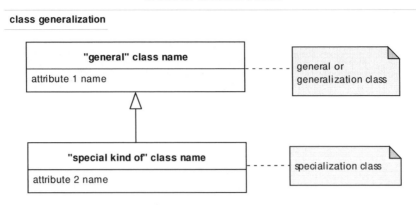

**(just the line from the specialization Class icon to the general Class icon)**

| | |
|---|---|
| Informal definition | A relationship in which the specialization class[22] contains all the properties (associations and attributes) of the generalization class[23], (the one pointed to by the triangle), plus more that are unique to it and do not apply to the generalization class. The generalization Class icon is pointed to by the triangle. For example, if you have two classes, Motor Vehicle and Motorcycle, since a motorcycle is "a special kind of" Motor Vehicle, a generalization relationship between the two would have the triangle pointing to the Motor Vehicle. |
| Used in diagrams | Class, Use Case |
| Suggestions for use | Create a generalization class when there are some classes where most of the properties (attributes, and associations) are identical, but some of the specialization classes have some different properties, or when there are just a few identical classes and visually displaying them all on a diagram helps your readers to verify you've identified them all. This option makes the different types visually explicit and clearly illustrates their differences. However it does increase the size of the diagram. See the generalization item in the How-to-Model Tips section of Chapter 8 Class Models for additional information. |

---

[22] known in data modeling as a subtype

[23] known in data modeling as a supertype

| Diagram examples | Figure 2-1 UML diagram categories, the arrow from the Structure Diagram class to the UML Diagram class, the arrow from the Behavior Diagram class to the UML Diagram class. Note that while they represent two separate generalization relationships and could be represented by two totally separate arrow lines, the lines were merged into a single arrowhead: that's a simplified and typical way of representing multiple generalization relationships to the same Class icon on a UML diagram. |
|---|---|

## Diagram Example

Figure 19-1 vehicle registration, Data Model diagram, a business perspective data model diagram, indicates that a *vehicle owner* has the following attributes (sometimes known as data elements in the non-UML world): a *name* with a datatype of *name-other*, a *street address* with a datatype of *text*, a *city name* with a datatype of *name-other*, a *state code* with the datatype of *code*, and a *zip code* with the datatype of *code*. A *vehicle owner owns* one or more *motor vehicles* (*1..\** is the multiplicity indicating a minimum lower bound of 1 and an upper bound of unlimited). Reading the association in the reverse direction indicates that a *motor vehicle* is *owned* by exactly one *vehicle owner*. Our fictitious Somestate Dept of Motor Vehicles allows only a single owner. A *motor vehicle* can have one or many *motor vehicle registrations* (The Somestate Dept of Motor Vehicles has a business rule that a new motor vehicle registration is issued each time a motor vehicle is purchased.). A *vehicle registration* is *paid for* by one or more *payments* (each renewal of a vehicle registration requires a payment). Each *payment pays for* exactly one *vehicle registration* (merely to keep the models simple, vehicle owners are not allowed to pay for two vehicle registrations with a single payment).

Note that the class and attribute names match the attribute names in the corresponding Figure 8-1 vehicle registration, UML Class diagram and Figure 9-1 vehicle registration, UML Object diagram.

## Diagram Tips

- All of the same tips noted for Class models in Chapter 8 Class Models apply, except that regular associations should always be used instead of aggregation and composition.

class vehicle registration

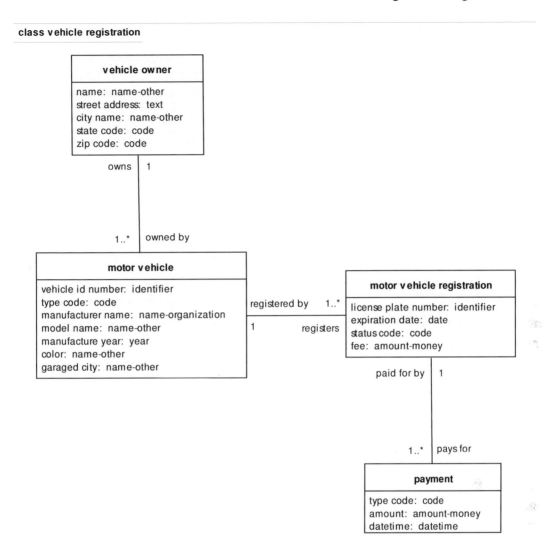

**Figure 19-1 vehicle registration, Data Model diagram**

## *How-to-Model Tips*

- Go for breadth first, then depth. Thus identify the most important classes first, then their most important relationships, followed by their most important attributes. Next, add the remainder of the classes, relationships, and attributes, then add the text definitions to each class and attribute, and optionally assign an analysis datatype to each attribute.[24]

- For business or domain models, look for items important to the business. These are typically the people, organizations, places, things, and events.

- Typically, the "event classes" (e.g., appointment, conference, contract, meeting, performance, sale) are the central focus of data models created for business analysis purposes.

- Frequently it's the role or the way the person or organization or place or thing participates in the event that's important, rather than just a person or organization or place or thing. For example, licensee and owner are the important concepts in a motor vehicle registry model, while person and organization could be considered to be the classes that might be included to play those roles.

- For associations, always use association role names (and never use association names).

- Harvest the classes from the project glossary, the direct object phrase portion of use case names, and the Action and Object Node names in your Activity diagrams.

- Harvest the attributes from your project glossary and your use case text.

- Harvest status attribute values from your State Machine states and Timing diagram states.

- To add additional information and be more precise, categorize each attribute using a standard set of analysis datatypes such as those described in Appendix C Analysis Datatypes.

- For those interested in an excellent introduction to data modeling, see [Hoberman, 2009]. For those interested in a brief overview, see [Ambler, Data Modeling 101].

---

[24] When you find there's confusion about a class or attribute, immediately create a draft definition for it, and for attributes list several representative attribute values. That frequently removes the confusion. However, creating high quality definitions can take a fair amount of time, particularly if multiple groups need to approve the definitions and that can impede forward progress on the model. That's why the author recommends not attempting to finalize definitions near the beginning of the modeling process.

- Generalization guidance. There are several options for representing generalization. Three alternative methods are described in the How-to-Model Tips section of Chapter 8 Class Models.

## Naming Guidelines

- The same naming conventions as those used for classes, attributes, and association role names for Class models in Chapter 8 Class Models are applicable to data models.
- David Hay explains in [Hay, 2011] how UML association role names should be reinterpreted for data modeling. However, that distinction is not critical for business analysts creating data models for business analysis purposes.

## Modeling Process Summary

The following is both a general process you may use as well as the process used to create the data model diagram in the next section.

The "Compare with related UML diagrams and adjust as appropriate" item in the following list is written under the assumption that you are creating a comprehensive and detailed model including all the UML diagram types and that you wish to have concepts covered in multiple diagram types whenever applicable. Thus suggestions such as "Confirm that all of the Lifeline icons in Sequence and Communication diagrams are represented as Actor icons in the Use Case diagrams. Add any missing Actor icons." may not apply in your situation.

1. List all of the persistent data elements.
   o Harvest these from the direct object phrases in Use Case names, from nouns in use case text, from Object Node icons in Activity diagrams, and from terms in a project glossary.
   o Include example value(s).
   o Categorize each data element into an analysis datatype, as defined in `Table C 1 Analysis Datatypes`.
   o Create an initial definition for each data element.
2. Place each data element under an appropriate data element category. See the Data Element List, Partial Example section of Chapter 8 Class Models for an example.
3. Give each data element category a class name.
4. Draw the diagram.

        o  Add each Class icon and its attributes. Be certain to add the definition for each class and attribute.

        o  Add any Generalization icons between each generalization Class icon and its specialization Class icons.

        o  Identify and add the Association icons between the Class icons.

        o  Add the association role name and multiplicity on each end of the association.

5.  If the diagram will ever be viewed without its context information (current or future system, perspective, author, date created or last updated), add a UML Note icon similar to that in `Figure 3-1 UML Note`.

6.  Compare it to related UML diagrams and adjust as appropriate:

        o  Check if any direct object phrases from use case names are missing as Class icons. Check if any nouns from use case text should be added as attributes in Classes.

        o  Check if any Object Nodes from Activity diagrams are missing as classes.

        o  Confirm that all of the attributes in the Object diagram are included as attributes in the corresponding classes.

        o  Check if the status attributes whose values are represented by State icons in State Machine models or Timing diagrams are present in the appropriate class in the data model.

        o  Check if any classes in a Class model are missing from the data model.

7.  Review and verify the model with the appropriate stakeholders.

## *Case Study Example Diagram*

Here is an example of how you might describe the following business perspective data model diagram to your stakeholders, reading counterclockwise from the top left.

The diagram includes the persistent data stored in the Somecity Train System.

A *train pass reader* has a *serial number* that is used as an *identifier*.

A *train pass* has a *current monetary value*.

A *train pass reader* can *read* from zero to many *train passes*. A *train pass* is *used in* from zero to many *train pass readers*.

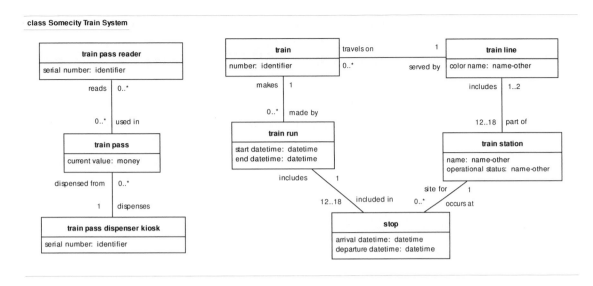

**Figure 19-2 case study, Data Model diagram, Somecity Train System**

A *train pass dispenser kiosk* has a *serial number* that is used as an *identifier*.

A *train pass* is *dispensed from* exactly one *train pass dispenser kiosk*. A *train pass dispenser kiosk dispenses* from zero to many *train passes*.

A *train* has a *number* that is used as an *identifier*.

A *train run* has a *start datetime* and an *end datetime*.

A *train makes* from zero to many *train runs*. A *train run* is *made by* exactly one *train*.

A *stop* has an *arrival datetime* and a *departure datetime*.

A *train run includes* from one to eighteen *stops*. A *stop* is *included in* exactly one *train run*.

A *train station* has a *name* and an *operational status*.

A *train station* is the *site for* from zero to many *train stops*. A *stop occurs at* exactly one *train station*.

A *train line* has a *color name*.

A *train line includes* between twelve and eighteen *train stations*. A *train station* is *part of* one to two *train lines*.

A *train line* is *served by* zero to many *trains*. A *train travels on* exactly one *train line*.

## *Relationship to UML Diagrams*

- An entity (represented by a Class icon when using the UML Class model notation) may be represented as a class in a Class model, as the direct object phrase portion of a use case name, as the nouns in use case text, and as Object Nodes in an Activity diagram

- An attribute in a data model may be represented as an attribute in a Class model or, alternatively, as an operation in a Class model (e.g., the attribute Motor Vehicle Registration.fee in a data model could be represented by the operation Motor Vehicle Registration.calculate fee in a Class model, rather than as an attribute in that Class model) or may be found as nouns in use case text.

- "Status" attributes may be the subject of a State Machine model or Timing diagram.

- The values of a "status" attribute may be represented as states in a State Machine model or Timing diagram.

- Some associations between classes may be indicated by the communication of a Message icon in a Sequence or Communication diagram.

"Where do I start?" you may be thinking. "There are too many choices." Here are some guidelines, illustrated first as two tables containing text, then as a sequence of three Activity diagrams. The following chapter describes the modeling process and associated decisions for the case study.

Near the beginning of your requirements process:

| If you: | then create: |
|---|---|
| need to visualize the various systems and actors and a list of the data categories exchanged | a Context diagram |
| need to visualize an overview of a process | an Activity diagram at an overview level |
| need to visualize the events the system or business needs to support | Use Case diagram(s) |
| need to partition a (typically large) model into smaller portions | a Package diagram |

Then:

| If you: | then create: |
|---|---|
| need to document the details of the user/system interactions | the text portion of your Use Case model |
| need to visually illustrate processes or user/system interactions | one or more Activity diagrams at a detailed level |
| need to visually illustrate the time sequence of interactions between systems and/or users | one or more Sequence diagrams<br><br>Alternatively, you may have captured that information in the form of use case text or in Activity diagrams. |
| need to visually summarize interactions between the various systems, optionally indicating their time sequence | a summary Communication diagram |
| find that the alternatives of Activity and Sequence diagrams won't suffice | an Interaction Overview diagram |

| If you: | then create: |
|---|---|
| need to visually illustrate the data categories and data elements and the operations performed on those data categories | a Class model |
| need to visually illustrate the persistent data that the system needs to support | a data model |
| need to visually illustrate in a concrete fashion any Class diagrams or data models you have previously created with actual data values | one or more Object diagrams |
| hear the word "status" or need to illustrate a lifecycle visually | a State Machine diagram for each non-trivial status code or set of related statuses |
| need to illustrate the time duration or time constraints between various statuses or events, and after you've created your State Machine diagrams | a Timing diagram |
| need a Composite Structure diagram, Component diagram, or Deployment diagram | nothing; let the software designers and developers create these diagrams |

The following Activity diagrams illustrate a process for creating UML diagrams for a project, first at an overview level, then at a more detailed level.

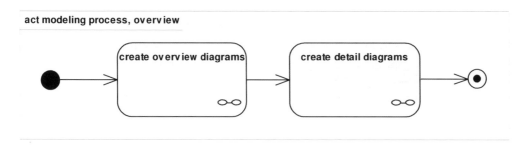

Figure 20-1 modeling process, UML Activity diagram, overview

**act modeling process, create overview diagrams**

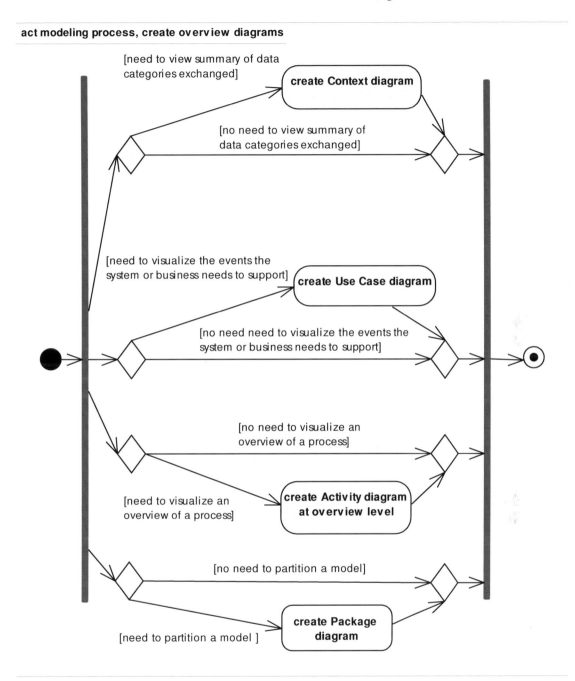

**Figure 20-2 modeling process, UML Activity diagram, create overview diagrams**

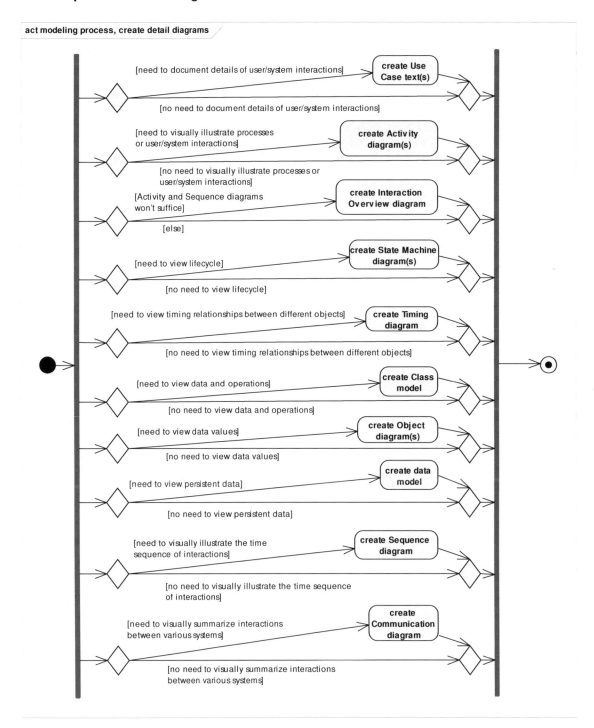

**Figure 20-3 modeling process, UML Activity diagram, create detail diagrams**

This chapter presents a case study for the fictitious Somecity Train System. It describes the context and process used for creating the diagrams and models, and highlights the relationships between aspects of the different models.

For this fictitious project, one portion of the business analysis team provided the UML diagrams and models portion of the requirements as presented in this chapter. Other business analysts are providing the remainder of the requirements, not included in this chapter.

## Case Study Overview

The Somecity Train System operates trains that transport passengers between train stations throughout the city and its surrounding cities and towns. The Somecity Train System has four train lines, each referred to by its color. They cross in a T-shape near the center of the city, so four of the train stations each serve two different train lines. All of the trains serving a given line are painted in that train line's color. A train run begins at the train stop at one end of a train line and ends at the train stop at the other end of the train line, making stops at all the train stations in between.

To ride a train requires that passengers purchase a train pass (similar to a credit card, except it is only valid for travel on the Somecity Train System) from a train pass dispenser kiosk. Passengers must swipe their train pass in the train pass reader to enter the gate of a train station. The train pass reader debits the amount of the train ride fare from the available amount stored on the train pass.

The Somecity Train System will create a web site that allows people to view train schedules and view any schedule delays on a train line.

## Case Study Modeling Process

To begin this project, the business analyst first decided to create a Context diagram of the future system. This provided an overview of the planned system in the form of a simple diagram illustrating the different systems involved and the people roles that will utilize the system. The diagram included the new Somecity Train System, and a credit card processor system (allowing passengers to purchase and add value to their train pass using credit cards in addition to cash). The diagram also included the people roles that will interact with the new system, identified as a web site visitor and a passenger, as well as the categories of data elements they exchange with the system.

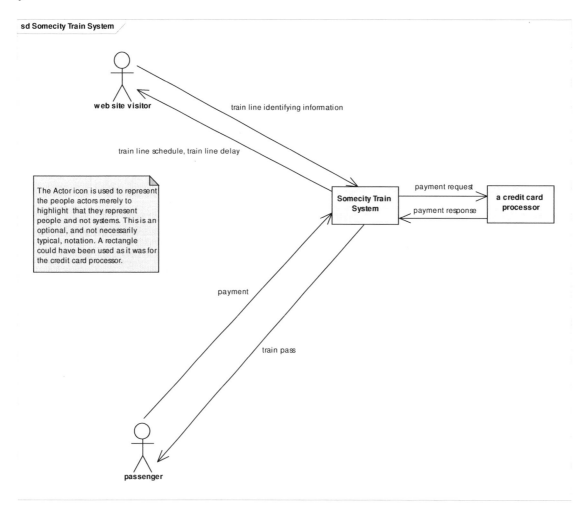

**Figure 21-1 case study, UML Context diagram, Somecity Train System**

Next, the business analyst decided to create a Use Case diagram to visually illustrate the different functions the new system must provide and the people roles and other systems involved in each function. The Context diagram provided the initial set of actors.

In a meeting facilitated by the business analysts, the subject matter experts identified initial use cases by asking what each of the actors wanted the system to accomplish. The train passenger wanted to purchase a train pass so that they could ride a train to their destination. A web site visitor wanted to view the train schedule for a train line so they could plan their trip to the airport. The business analyst created an initial Use Case diagram and reviewed it with the subject matter experts. During the review, the subject matter experts identified additional use cases. The subject matter experts indicated a web site visitor should be able to view any delays on a train line so that they could plan their trip or make alternate travel arrangements. The subject matter experts indicated that passengers should also be able to add additional amounts to their train passes.

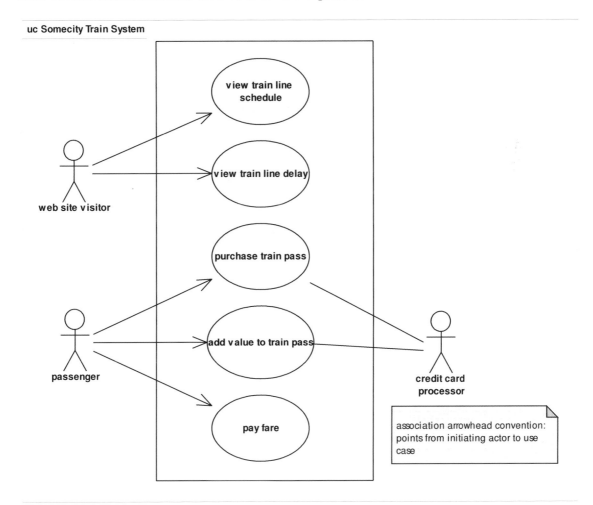

**Figure 21-2 case study, UML Use Case diagram, Somecity Train System: system use case**

Note that all of the Actor names in the Use Case diagram matched the external entity names in the Context diagram.

Next, for the first use case to be written, the business analyst created the use case text for the main success scenario for the Purchase Train Pass use case.

Use Case Name: **Purchase Train Pass**

Use Case Category: system

Goal: buy train pass

Primary Actor: passenger

Secondary Actor(s): credit card processor

**Main Success Scenario**

1. The passenger indicates they want to purchase a train pass.
2. The system presents the train pass amount choices.
3. The passenger indicates the pass amount.
4. The system presents payment instructions.
5. The passenger inserts the appropriate monetary amount into the train pass dispenser kiosk.
6. The system validates that the currency entered are US currency amounts acceptable to the system.
7. The system records the payment.
8. The system issues the train pass.
9. The system presents "take pass" instructions.
10. The system prints a payment receipt.
11. The system presents the available options for the next passenger's use

The Chief Customer Officer wanted to see an overview of a passenger taking a train trip from the business perspective, since that is the most frequent process the system supports. The business analyst created an overview Activity diagram of that business process.

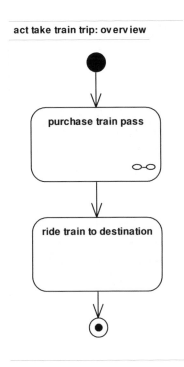

**Figure 21-3 case study, UML Activity diagram, take trip overview**

Note that the first Activity in that overview Activity diagram had the same name as the corresponding Use Case.

The Chief Customer Officer wanted to review the purchase train pass activity in more detail, and knowing that she preferred diagrams, the business analyst created an Activity diagram of just the main success scenario of the Purchase Train Pass use case for her review.

Note that the Activity Partitions in the Activity diagram matched the Actor names in the Use Case diagram, and the external systems and people roles names from the Context diagram. Also, the Action names in the Activity diagram matched the verb and direct object phrase names in the steps of the use case text.

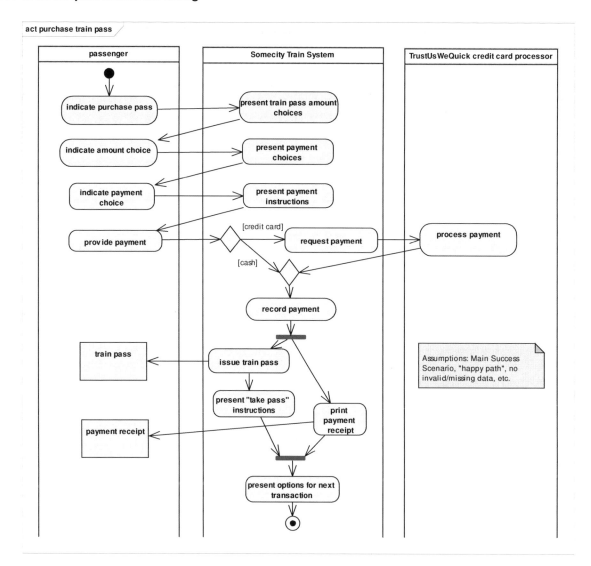

**Figure 21-4 case study, UML Activity diagram, purchase train pass details**

In a meeting, a group of subject matter experts used the Activity diagram to review the actions and identify the most important extension conditions of the Purchase Train Pass use case:

- The passenger inserted too much money.
- The passenger didn't insert enough money.
- The passenger inserted unacceptable denominations (e.g., $100 bill).
- The credit card payment was not accepted.
- The passenger did not remove their purchased train pass from the train pass dispenser kiosk.

Later, the business analyst worked with the subject matter experts to add all of the use case steps to resolve all of the identified extension conditions.

The group felt that the Chief Financial Officer would benefit from an overview that focused on the credit card usage for purchasing a train pass, the most frequent path through the use case, so the business analysts created an Interaction Overview diagram of the Purchase Train Pass use case.

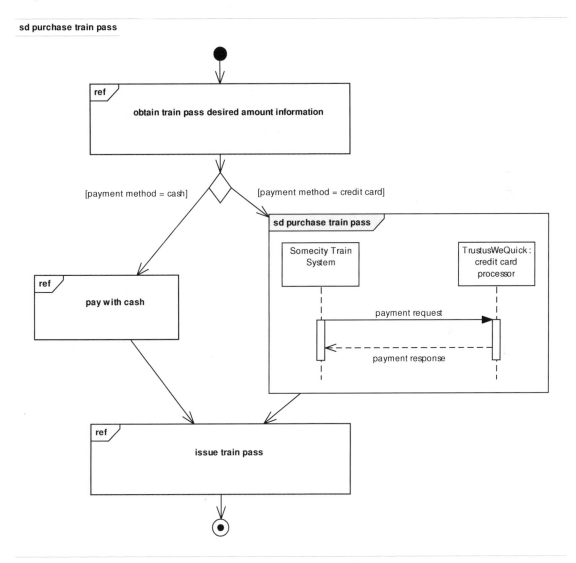

**Figure 21-5 case study, UML Interaction Overview diagram, purchase train pass overview**

Note that the Interaction Use *purchase train pass* in the Interaction Overview diagram matched the Activity name in the Activity diagram and the Use Case icon name in the Use Case diagram.

The Operations Manager was concerned about making certain the train maintenance process would be handled properly, since there are state regulations that need to be followed. Together with the business analyst, they created a State Machine model that illustrated where the train maintenance process fit in. The Operations Manager noted several business rules, which were then added to the draft version, some as guard conditions on state transitions: newly delivered trains were automatically placed in *maintenance* status, not *available* status, as the business analyst initially drew; in order to change the *train operation status* from *maintenance* to *available*, the train had to *pass the inspection test*; before an *in use* train is allowed to *return to the garage*, the train could have *no passengers*.

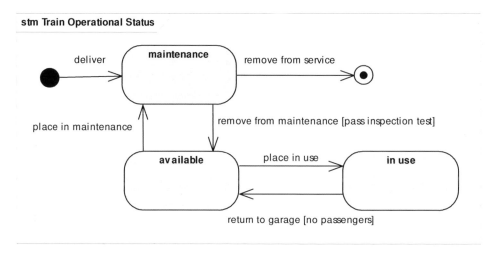

**Figure 21-6 case study, UML State Machine diagram, train operational status**

Since the new Trains would be driverless, the Safety Officer wanted to understand how safety concerns fit into the new system. The business analyst created the following Timing diagram to illustrate that.

The Safety Officer appreciated the timing constraints that were illustrated by the Timing Diagram.

The group then decided to analyze the data portion of the project in detail. They collected all of the data elements that would be needed per use case into spreadsheets. The data categories, data element names, etc. were all preliminary and would be enhanced later, when translated into a Class model.

**sd Train Movement and Door Operation**

Figure 21-7 case study, UML Timing diagram, train movement and door operation status

Table 21-1 Data Element List, Case Study, partial text example

| Data Category | Data Element Name | Example Values | Analysis Datatype |
|---|---|---|---|
| Train | number | 16389 | identifier |
| Run | start time | 4:50 pm | time |
| | end time | 5:55 pm | time |
| Stop | arrival time | 5:25 pm | time |
| | departure time | 5:27 pm | time |
| station | name | Davis Square, Alewife | name-other |
| | status | Open, closed | code |
| line | color | Red | name-other |
| pass | amount | $10.00 | money |
| pass reader | serial number | DOT15289 | identifier |
| pass dispenser | serial number | DOT20642 | identifier |

The business analyst then organized the data elements and data element categories into a Class model, obtained definitions for all of the attributes, and added the operations. The following Class diagram is the result of the review of the draft Class diagram with the stakeholders.

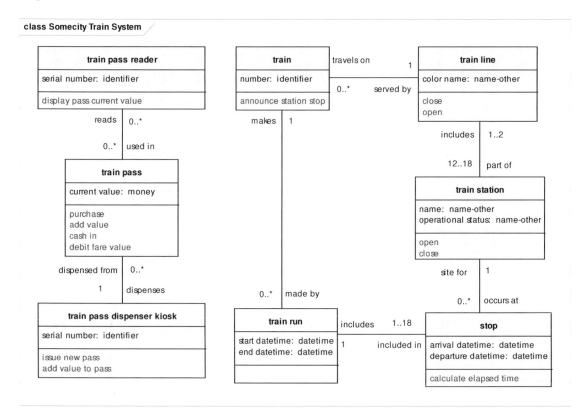

**Figure 21-8 case study, UML Class diagram, Somecity Train System**

Note that the attributes in the Class diagram matched the noun names in the use case text.

The definitions of the classes and attributes contained in the Class diagram are included in the following table.

**Table 21-2 Class Model Data Definitions, Case Study, partial text example**

| Class name | Attribute name | Definition |
|---|---|---|
| train pass dispenser kiosk | | A device that issues a Somecity Train System train pass after receiving payment for the train pass. |
| | serial number | The serial number assigned to a train pass dispenser kiosk by the manufacturer. |
| train pass reader | | A device that reads Somecity Train System train passes and debits the amount of the train ride from the available balance amount on the train pass. |
| | serial number | The serial number assigned to a train pass reader by the manufacturer. |
| stop | | The stopping of a train at a train station to allow passengers to disembark and board the train. |
| | arrival datetime | The actual date and time a train arrived at a train station (e.g., 1/26/2012 5:50 am). |
| | departure datetime | The actual date and time a train departed from a train station (e.g., 1/26/2012 5:51 am). |
| train | | A series of up to six train cars coupled together that travels along a train line to transport passengers. |
| | number | The serial number assigned by the manufacturer of a train in the Somecity Train System to the first of the train cars coupled together to provide train service along a train line. |
| | operational status | A categorization of operational status of the train (e.g., maintenance, available, in use). |
| train line | | A series of train stations joined by train tracks allowing a train to transport passengers between the stations of the train line. |
| | color name | The name of the color of the train line (e.g., Red, Blue). |
| train run | | One occurrence of a train running from one end stop on a train line to the other end stop of that train line. |
| | start datetime | The actual start date and time of a train run (e.g., 1/26/2012 5:45 am). |
| | end datetime | The actual end date and time of a train run (e.g., 1/26/2012 6:32 am). |
| train station | | A train station of the Somecity Train System. |
| | name | The name of the train station (e.g., Braintree, Alewife). |
| | operational status | A categorization of the operational status of the train station (e.g., open, closed). |
| train pass | | A credit-card like device that can be used to pay for a train ride on the Somecity Train System. |
| | current value | The current value of the train pass in U.S. dollars (e.g., $7.50). |

For a review with subject matter experts from the Operations Department, the business analyst created an Object diagram of a portion of a train run to make the Class diagram more concrete for the subject matter experts.

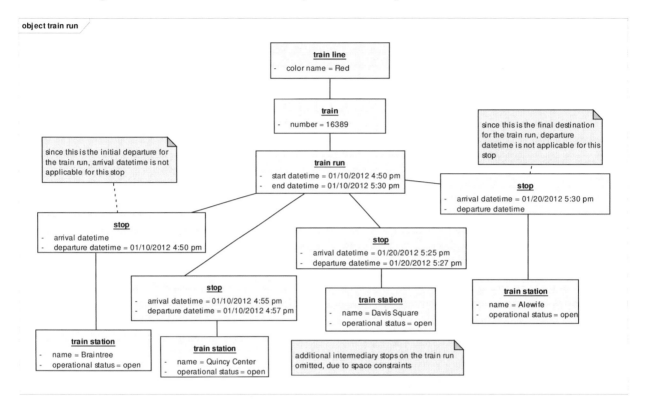

**Figure 21-9 case study, UML Object diagram, train run**

Note that the class names and attribute names in the Object diagram matched those in the Class diagram.

Since there was a data modeler on the project, there was no need to create a data model. The data modeler indicated she would use the information from the Class diagram to create a data model for the database design as part of the design process.

There was concern about the credit card processing aspect of the system, so the business analyst investigated one of the credit card processing systems being considered and created a Sequence diagram to illustrate the message exchanges involved. When reviewing the Sequence diagram, the Chief Marketing Officer indicated there should be a time limit of five seconds between the time the system sent a credit card payment request and received the credit card payment response. The business analyst added that constraint to the Sequence diagram.

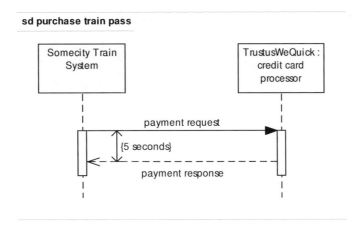

**Figure 21-10 case study, UML Sequence diagram, purchase train pass: main success scenario**

Note that the lifeline names in the Sequence diagram matched the Actor names in the Use Case diagram and the external entity names in the Context diagram, and the Activity Partition names in the Activity diagram.

Since the credit card processing system was the only external system, the business analyst determined that there was no need to create a Communication diagram; the Sequence diagram was clear and simple enough that there was no reason to create another view of the information exchanges between the two systems.

Since the business analyst team is only responsible for requirements and not design, they decided there was no need for Composite Structure, Component, or Deployment diagrams.

The business analyst recognized that there were three distinct groups of stakeholders and decided to divide the entire model into three packages so that they could produce a set of requirements diagrams and models for each of the three groups. The following is the Package diagram that illustrates the three packages.

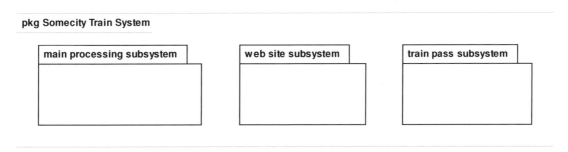

**Figure 21-11 case study, UML Package diagram, Somecity Train System**

Together with the other requirements, the appropriate stakeholders reviewed the contents of the three Packages of UML diagrams and models. The business stakeholders agreed that a system meeting the requirements documented would meet their needs, the software development team agreed that the full set of requirements would allow them to design the system, and the testing team agreed that the full set of requirements was sufficient for them to create an initial test plan, and to identify and begin specifying many of the test cases. The project sponsor was pleased that she could review just the overview portion of the requirements. The requirements were approved.

The project sponsor thanked the business analyst team for producing a clear, concise, consistent, and complete set of requirements.

**A Guide to the Business Analysis Body of Knowledge (BABOK)**: a document published by the International Institute of Business Analysis that describes the practice of business analysis.

**Actor**: the role of a person or an external system or device that interacts with the system or business or component under analysis. See also **initiating actor**, **primary actor**.

**Activity partition:** a bounded portion of an Activity diagram used to segregate the group of Actions, Activities, Decisions, etc. performed by a single actor. Also known as a swimlane or partition.

**Alternate path**: see **extension**.

**BABOK**: see **A Guide to the Business Analysis Body of Knowledge**.

**BPMN**: see **Business Process Modeling Notation**.

**Basic path**: see **main success scenario**.

**Business Actor**: a person (or role of a person) participating in a business use case. See also **actor**, **business use case**.

**Business Analysis Body of Knowledge**: see **A Guide to the Business Analysis Body of Knowledge**.

**Business Process Modeling Notation (BPMN)**: a standard notation for business process modeling, officially known as Business Process Model and Notation (BPMN), that is maintained by the Object Management Group (OMG).

**Business Rule**: a statement that defines or constrains an aspect of a business. It contains the terms, facts, derivations, and action assertions of relevance to the business (e.g., if ... then ... statements).

**Business Use Case**: a category of use cases whose focus is the business processes of an organization, and not a software system.

**Compartment**: a portion of a Class icon separated by horizontal line(s) from the other portions. The top compartment contains the class name, the middle compartment contains the attribute names, and the bottom compartment contains the operation names.

**Component**: a collection of software that can be installed and replaced as a unit.

**Component Use Case**: a category of use cases whose focus is a single component of a software system.

**Composite State**: a state that contains other states. Referred to in this book as **superstate**. The contained states are referred to as **substates**. Contrast with **substate**.

**Domain**: the business area (e.g. marketing, real estate) undergoing analysis; the specification of the allowable values for an attribute in a data model (as used in data modeling). For a coded attribute, the attribute domain often takes the form of a list of allowable values or, alternatively, a reference to a list.

**Extend**: a relationship between two use cases where the main use case (known as the "extended" use case) is extended by another use case (known as the "extending" use case). One usage of extending use cases is to provide optional behavior for the main use case.

**Extension**: an other than normal condition (e.g., an alternative action an actor could take, an error condition the system detects, such as "date of birth in the future", or "invalid license plate number") for a use case step and the sequence of use case steps that then follow the detection of that condition and lead to its resolution, successful or unsuccessful. Instead of the term extension, some use different terms, depending on whether the use case steps end in success (sometimes called alternate success situation or alternate flow) or failure (sometimes called exception or failure situation). Not to be confused with the Extend use case relationship or Extension Point.

**Extension Point**: a name for a step in a main (extended) use case, at which point an extending use case begins. See the Extend portion of `Table 5-1 Use Case Diagram Notation` for an example of how these display in Use Case diagrams.

**Flow**: the sequence of steps or actions.

**Frame**: an icon that appears as a rectangle with an embedded rectangle with its bottom right corner cutoff in the upper left corner that optionally contains a frame heading. It may optionally be used to enclose the elements of any UML diagram. It is also used in Interaction Overview diagrams to embed a Sequence diagram or

Communication diagram or Timing diagram or another Interaction Overview diagram as an Interaction.

**Frame heading**: the text portion of a frame that includes the UML frame kind name or abbreviation followed by the diagram name.

**Frame kind abbreviation**: a short alphabetic code for a frame kind name (e.g., uc representing use case) that may be displayed in a frame heading. See `Table 3-1 UML Frame Kinds` for a complete list.

**Frame kind name**: the name of a UML diagram type or category (e.g., Use Case, State Machine) that may be displayed in a frame heading. See `Table 3-1 UML Frame Kinds` for a complete list.

**Functional requirement**: A category of requirement that represents the actions the system must perform. Contrast this with non-functional requirement.

**General value lifeline**: one of two diagram formats of a Timing diagram. In this version, the state values are displayed as six-sided diamond figures. Compare this to **State or condition timeline** format.

**Guard condition**: An expression that evaluates to either true or false. Used in Activity diagrams to control flow and in State Machine models to control state transitions.

**Guillemet**: a special type of quotation mark used in UML models to enclose UML keywords and stereotypes, «keyword». Although guillemets are special symbols, they are frequently written using the less than and greater than signs, <<not true guillemet>>.

**Include**: a relationship between two use cases where steps are removed from the main use case (known as the "including" use case) and placed in a separate use case (known as the "included" use case). This may be done when those steps are common to multiple use cases and are factored out to the "included" use case to avoid duplication across the multiple use cases.

**Initiating actor**: the actor that performs the first step in the use case. This is typically also the primary actor. There may be no initiating actor when the system itself initiates the use case, typically based on time (e.g., end of day, month end close). See also **actor**, **primary actor**.

**Interaction**: a general term representing an information exchange between two entities (where an entity can be a person, a hardware device (e.g., kiosk), or a software system); a category of UML diagram types (Communication, Interaction Overview, Sequence, and Timing diagrams); a UML diagram icon that illustrates a contained Sequence diagram (or one of the other UML Interaction category diagram types).

**Keyword**: a reserved word that has a special meaning when it is used in a UML diagram (e.g., datastore, include). On a UML diagram, they're enclosed in guillemets (e.g., «include» is displayed on an include association in a UML Use Case diagram to distinguish it from a regular association). The following table lists the UML keywords that would be used for business analysis purposes together with the UML icon and diagrams on which they could appear.

Table A-1 UML Keywords Used in Business Analysis

| Keyword | UML icon and diagrams |
|---------|----------------------|
| component | Component on Component diagram |
| datastore | Datastore Node on Activity diagram |
| device | Node on Deployment diagram |
| document | Artifact deployed on Node on Deployment diagram |
| extend | Extend association on Use Case diagram |
| include | Include association on Use Case diagram |
| iterative | Expansion region on Activity diagram |
| parallel | Expansion region on Activity diagram |
| stream | Expansion region on Activity diagram |

**Lifeline**: an individual participant (frequently referred to as interacting entity) in an information exchange. Typically it represents a system, although it could represent people roles when modeling user/system interactions. Used in Sequence and Communication diagrams.

**Main success scenario**: The one sequence of use case steps, from beginning to end, where everything goes correctly and the use case ends in success with the actor achieving their goal. Also known as basic path, main steps, and "happy path". Compare this with **Extension**. See also **scenario**.

**Model**: (a) a representation of a software system or business. A model can consist of multiple diagram types with their associated text. (b) all of the diagrams of a specific diagram type with their associated text (e.g., the Use Case model for a system). This definition is only used in this book when referring to Use Case, Class, and State Machine models, since those most frequently utilize more than one diagram for a software system or business. (c) a specific diagram type and its associated text (e.g., a single Class diagram with its associated text). (d) the process of creating a model.

**Non-functional requirement**: a category of requirement representing the qualities a system should have (e.g., performance capabilities, security capabilities, usability characteristics). Contrast this with **functional requirement**.

**Note**: see **UML Note**.

**Partition**: see **Activity Partition**.

**People roles**: a term used to categorize how people are interacting with the system (or business) under analysis. For example, passenger, registration administrator, web site visitor. It is used in this book to distinguish people actors from system and device actors. See also **actor**.

**Perspective**: a viewpoint. For example, a model of a business could be created for business analysis purposes, while a different model of the system that the business uses or will use could be created for system design purposes. Those would be two different perspectives. The Zachman Framework for Enterprise Architecture [Zachman] is one framework that defines these different perspectives.

**Primary actor**: the actor that has the goal in a use case. This is typically also the initiating actor. See also **actor**, **initiating actor**

**Project Glossary**: a list of terms and their definitions that are important to the project. For many items, there are two definitions: a business definition and a technical definition. Trying to force both into the same definition is frequently counterproductive. For example, a business definition of a Vehicle Identification Number could be "a manufacturer assigned identifier for a motor vehicle", while a technical definition could be "an externally assigned 17-character alphanumeric identifier, valued uniquely for each instance of a motor vehicle in the agency's Motor Vehicle Registration database".

**Scenario**: one complete set of steps through a use case from start to termination. A scenario can result either in the success or failure of achieving the goal of the use case. Compare this with **main success scenario**. Be aware that some people use the term "scenario" for other meanings, including any user story.

**Simple state**: a state that does not contain other states. Contrast with **superstate.**

**Stakeholder**: in business analysis, a person or organization having an influence on the initiative or having interests that could be affected by the initiative.

**State Machine**: a synonym for a State Machine model.

**State or condition timeline**: one of two diagram formats of a Timing diagram. In this version, the state or condition values are represented as named horizontal levels of a horizontal line. Compare this to **General value lifeline** format.

**State transition**: The term used in this book to refer to the concept known in UML simply as Transition. see **Transition**.

**Stereotype:** a special type of keyword that has a predefined meaning in UML (e.g., «document», defined in the UML specification as "A generic file that is not a «source» file or «executable». Subclass of «file».").

**Substate**: a state that is contained in another state. Contrast with **superstate**.

**Superstate**: a state that contains other states. The contained states are referred to as **substates**. This encompasses the UML terms **composite state** and containing state. Contrast with **substate**.

**Swimlane**: see **Activity Partition**.

**System Use Case**: a category of use cases whose focus is a software system.

**Transition**: the UML term for the change of an object's status from a source state to a target state; or the Transition icon in a State Machine diagram that represents that change. Referred to in this book as **state transition**.

**Trigger Event**: The action that causes a state transition in a State Machine model. Referred to in UML simply as "event".

**UML**: see **Unified Modeling Language**.

**UML Note**: an icon containing a text annotation. Notes can be included in any UML diagram. See `Figure 3-1 UML Note` for an example.

**Unified Modeling Language (UML)**: a modeling language issued by the Object Management Group that includes diagram notation for use in modeling business data, business processes, and software systems.

**Use Case scenario**: see **scenario**.

**Use Case step**: A portion of a use case consisting of an action performed by either the system under analysis or an actor. Use case steps are typically represented as text statements in the text version of a use case. They may also be represented using an Activity diagram with each use case step being represented by one or more Action icons or a portion of an Activity icon.

**Use Case text**: a text description of the sequence of steps between the system and its various actors, including people actors, devices, and other systems. Contrast with a Use Case diagram.

**Zachman Framework for Enterprise Architecture (Zachman Framework)** [Zachman]: an architectural framework that differentiates between the different perspectives of business and system.

**Zachman Framework2** [Zachman]: the most recent version of the Zachman Framework for Enterprise Architecture.

Little did I realize at the time that so much of the grammar I learned from my seventh and eighth grade English teacher, Mrs. Rogers, would be so helpful in modeling! I never thought I'd be recommending that modelers around the world use gerunds for naming states, active voice verbs in the present tense followed by a direct object phrase for naming use cases, singular noun phrases for naming classes, etc. For those of you who weren't fortunate enough to have Mrs. Rodgers as your English teacher, this summary of the grammatical terms used in the Naming Guidelines section of previous chapters, as well as examples of each of these terms, will save you the time of reading a book on English grammar just to improve the quality of your models.

- adjective
  - o Examples: <u>city</u> name (versus just name); <u>model</u> name (versus just name); <u>motor</u> vehicle (versus just vehicle); <u>vehicle</u> registration (versus just registration). In each of these cases, the initial underlined adjective is used to make the noun phrase more specific than just the noun itself. While there are many types of vehicles, including bicycles and scooters, the Somestate Dept of Motor Vehicles System is concerned with just motor vehicles.
  - o Use as part of a noun phrase when the noun needs to be qualified or made more specific.
- adverb
  - o Examples: always; frequently; generally; probably; quickly; rarely; seldom; sometimes; usually
  - o Don't use in use case text and avoid their use in requirements documents: they're vague and not testable.
- active voice verb
  - o Examples: make; discharge; own; pay for; renew; transfer
  - o Use for the initial part of a use case name.
  - o Use for operation names in a Class model.
  - o Use for trigger event names in a State Machine model.
- active voice verb followed by a direct object phrase, in the singular:
  - o Examples: add task to project plan, book flight reservation, cancel hotel reservation, generate monthly invoice, request laboratory test, reserve rental car

- o Use for Activity and Action icon names in an Activity diagram.
- o Use for use case names.
- direct object phrase
  - o Examples: make <u>flight reservation</u>; renew <u>motor vehicle registration</u>
  - o Use as the final part of a use case name.
  - o a noun phrase, underlined in the preceding two examples, used as the direct object of an active voice verb.
- gerund
  - o Examples: displaying; listening; moving; opening; running; starting; stopping; working
  - o Use either gerunds or past participles for states in a State Machine model.
  - o There are some verbs that are typically followed by gerunds, such as begin, continue, finish, and stop. The gerunds that follow these verbs tend to be good candidates for states in a State Machine model (e.g. continue <u>working</u>, finish <u>eating</u>, stop <u>shouting</u>).
- noun phrase
  - o Examples: customer; flight reservation; hotel reservation; library book; motor vehicle registration; purchaser
  - o Use as direct object phrase as part of use case names (singular, not plural).
  - o Use for actor names in the singular (not plural) form in Use Case models.
  - o Use for class names (singular, not plural).
  - o Use for attribute names (generally singular; use plural only to indicate that the attribute can occur multiple times and you adopt that convention, rather than displaying attribute multiplicity).
  - o Use for Activity Partition names in Activity diagrams.
  - o Use as guard conditions on outgoing flows of a decision in Activity diagrams.
  - o Use for package names.
- passive voice verb
  - o Examples (to not use): I was hit in the head by a falling tree branch; the letter was mailed by the child.
  - o Examples (to use): owned by; payed for by
  - o Use for association role names.
  - o Don't use in use case names or use case text; instead, use active voice verbs.

- o Avoid using in requirements text; instead, use active voice verbs.
- past participle
  - o Examples: completed; discharged; expired; revoked; stopped; suspended
  - o Use either past participles or gerunds for states in a State Machine model.
  - o Use as decision branch names (technically outgoing Control Flows from a Decision Node) in an Activity diagram (e.g., accepted, rejected).
- pronoun
  - o Examples: he; it; she; them; they
  - o Avoid using in use case text. Instead use the noun the pronoun refers to. This avoids confusion.
  - o Avoid using in requirement documents in general, for the same reason.
- proper noun
  - o Examples: International Institute of Business Analysis; John Paul Jones; Martin Luther King, Jr. National Memorial; North Carolina
  - o Use for node names in a Deployment diagram, actor names in a Use Case diagram, external entity names in a Context diagram, appropriate attribute values or Object names in an Object diagram (e.g., person, place, or thing names), lifeline names for external systems in Sequence and Communication diagrams.

Analysis Datatypes are a simple to use tool to categorize data elements that appear as attributes in your Class Models and data models during the analysis process. They help your subject matter experts to be clearer about their data requirements. By classifying attributes and data elements into one of the analysis datatypes, you'll improve the precision of your analysis work products, thus helping to reduce the likelihood of misunderstandings. Utilizing analysis datatypes will also assist your data modelers, and software and database designers.

**Table C-1 Analysis Datatypes**

| Datatype Name | Description | Example Value(s) | Sample attribute using the datatype |
|---|---|---|---|
| indicator | a two valued code set representing the values true/false or yes/no; also known as Boolean | yes; no | hazardous material indicator |
| code | a constrained value set typically used for categorizing something | M (representing male); F (representing female) | gender code |
| datetime | a point in time | 11/9/2008 9:09 pm | accident date and time |
| date | a specific date in time | January 28, 2009 | birth date |
| time | a specific time of day | 5:30 pm | appointment time |
| money | a monetary amount, including the unit of currency | $4.35 US dollars | payment amount |
| amount | a measured or observed amount, including the units; you may want to subcategorize amounts into distance, time, weight, etc., as was done for monetary amounts | 2.1 meters | height |
| quantity | a count of individual items such as people, places, and things | 47 | attendee count |

| Datatype Name | Description | Example Value(s) | Sample attribute using the datatype |
|---|---|---|---|
| sequence number | a specific position within an ordinal ranking (e.g., by time, by importance) | 2 | birth order |
| percentage | the ratio between two amounts having the same units or between two quantities of the same type of items, expressed as a percentage | 75% | current year cost increase |
| (postal) address | a street or post office box address | 123 Main St, Mayberry, NC 27030, USA | work address |
| phone number | a telephone number; includes phone, fax, and pager numbers | +1 (617) 555-1212 | work phone |
| email address | an electronic mail address | MeMyselfAndI@gmail.com | personal email address |
| internet address | a web address, Uniform Resource Locator | www.iiba.org | web address |
| name-person | a name of a human being | John Paul Jones | spouse name |
| name-organization | a name of an organization | IIBA Greater Boston Chapter | chapter name |
| name-other | a name of something other than a person or organization | Monthly Chapter Meeting | meeting name |
| identifier | a value that uniquely distinguishes one instance from all others | 1234 5678 9012 0000 | credit card number |
| specification text | a textual specification that could be broken down into distinct data elements[25] | Monday through Friday, 9:30 am to 5:30 pm | store hours |
| text | human readable text, frequently a description of something | When, in the course of human events, it becomes necessary ... | document text |

[25] Frequently used to specify schedules of various types (e.g., meeting schedules, class schedules, movie schedules, business hours)

| Datatype Name | Description | Example Value(s) | Sample attribute using the datatype |
|---|---|---|---|
| encoded data | a file, document, etc. that typically requires special software to unencode or view it | IIBA-logo.jpg | logo |
| ratio | a ratio between two amounts | 30 miles per hour | speed limit |

## How-to-Model Tips

To assign the appropriate Analysis Datatype to an attribute in a Class model or data model, begin at the top of the list, work your way down, and stop at the first applicable analysis datatype.

## Naming Guidelines

Use a short form of the analysis datatype as the suffix of most attribute names in a Class model or data model. For example, Organization.address, Material.hazardous material indicator, Person.gender code, SalesTax.percentage.

## Notes

The example values listed are intended to represent the logical contents, not necessarily the format of the data that's stored in a database or presented on a display. For example, an indicator may be stored in a database as 0, 1 or y, n; encoded data may contain a logo in JPG format, or a photograph; a date may be stored in one of various formats (e.g., 2011-08-17) and displayed in multiple formats (e.g., 8/17/2011, August 17, 2011).

The list is not intended to be exhaustive - you should extend it as needed. For example, the amount datatype could be specialized (based on various axes such as time, weight, length, or distance) into time amount, weight amount, length/distance amount, force amount, liquid measure amount, etc., as money was.

## Relationship to Other UML Diagrams

- Analysis Datatypes should be assigned to each attribute in a Class model and a data model. Since Object diagrams are typically derived from a corresponding Class model, they're also helpful in assigning values to the attributes in an Object diagram.

- The code datatype is typically appropriate for the Class or data model attribute that holds the states in a State Machine model and a Timing diagram.

[Ambler, Data Modeling 101] Ambler, Scott, Data Modeling 101, www.agiledata.org/essays/dataModeling101.html

A brief introduction to data modeling, illustrating multiple notations

[Ambler, A UML Profile for Data Modeling] Ambler, Scott, A UML Profile for Data Modeling, www.agiledata.org/essays/umlDataModelingProfile.html

A proposed UML Profile for data modeling.

[Blaha, 2010] Blaha, Michael, 2010, *Patterns of Data Modeling*, CRC Press

An advanced book on data modeling patterns.

[Burk, 2004] Burk, Susan, 2004, Business Rules and Objects: Blending the Best of Both Worlds, presentation to Boston Data Management Association

A presentation that described a method for noting business rules in use case text.

[Chisholm, 2010] Chisholm, Malcolm D., 2010, *Definitions in Information Management*, Design Media Publishing

An excellent book devoted to definitions.

[Coad, 1999] Coad, Peter, Lefebvre, E., DeLuca, J., 1999, *Java Modeling in Color with UML*, Upper Saddle River, NJ: Prentice Hall PTR

Don't be fooled by the title: this book presents an excellent method for categorizing both UML classes and data into patterns that recur over and over again. You don't have to know anything about Java to put these ideas to use. It's certainly not an introductory text, but the author recommends this for people who wish to explore Class models in more detail.

[Cockburn, 2001] Cockburn, Alistair, 2001, *Writing Effective Use Cases*, Upper Saddle River, NJ: Prentice Addison-Wesley

One of the first and still one of the best books about use cases.

[Fowler, 2004] Fowler, Martin, 2004, *UML Distilled: A Brief Guide to the Standard Object Modeling Language* (Third Edition), Boston, MA: Addison-Wesley

One of the first and still the best overview book about the Unified Modeling Language.

[Hay, 2011] Hay, David C, 2011, *UML and Data Modeling: A Reconciliation*, Technics Publications, LLC

An in-depth analysis of using UML Class model notation for data modeling.

[Hoberman, 2009] Hoberman, Steve, 2009, *Data Modeling Made Simple 2nd Edition, A Practical Guide for Business & Information Technology Professionals*, Technics Publications, LLC

A short but comprehensive introduction to data modeling.

[BABOK 2.0] International Institute of Business Analysis, *A Guide to the Business Analysis Body of Knowledge®* (BABOK® Guide), Version 2.0. Available at www.iiba.org

A standard for the practice of business analysis.

[Ross, 2010] Ross, Ronald, 2010, *Business Rule Concepts: Getting to the Point of Knowledge* (Third Edition), Business Rule Solutions, LLC

A comprehensive coverage of business rules.

[Schneider et al., 2001] Schneider, Geri and Winters, Jason P., 2001, *Applying Use Cases: A Practical Guide*, Addison-Wesley

This is my favorite book on use cases because it's written in an easy to understand manner and includes examples.

[UML Infrastructure 2.4.1] Object Management Group, *OMG Unified Modeling Language (OMG UML), Infrastructure*, Version 2.4.1, 2011

This is the portion of the UML specification that defines the scope of UML. It describes the language architecture and specification approach. Available at www.omg.org

[UML Superstructure 2.4.1] Object Management Group, *OMG Unified Modeling Language (OMG UML), Superstructure*, Version 2.4.1, 2011

This is the portion of the UML specification where a business analyst can find all the UML diagram elements. Available at www.omg.org

[von Halle, 2002] von Halle, Barbara, 2002, *Business Rules Applied: Building Better Systems Using the Business Rule Approach*, New York, NY: Wiley

An excellent introduction and overview to business rules.

[von Halle, 2009] von Halle, Barbara and Goldberg, Larry, 2009, *The Decision Model: A Business Logic Framework Linking Business and Technology*, New York, NY: Auerbach Publications/Taylor & Francis, LLC

An excellent method for documenting business decisions in conjunction with business rules.

[Zachman] Zachman Framework Associates, Zachman Framework2

An architectural framework helpful in understanding the different perspectives for models. Available at www.zachmanframeworkassociates.com